Militarizing the American Criminal Justice System

Advisor in Criminal Justice to Northeastern University Press
Gil Geis

Militarizing the American Criminal Justice System

The Changing Roles of the Armed Forces and the Police

Edited by Peter B. Kraska

Northeastern University Press
Boston

Northeastern University Press 2001

Library of Congress Cataloging-in-Publication Data

Militarizing the American criminal justice system : the changing roles of the Armed Forces and the police / edited by Peter B. Kraska.
    p.   cm.
  Includes bibliographical references and index.
  ISBN 1-55553-475-9 (pbk. : alk. paper) — ISBN 1-55553-476-7 (cloth: alk. paper)
      1. Law enforcement—United States   2. Corrections—United States.   3. Militarism—United States.   4. Police—United States.   5. Armed Forces—United States.   I.   Kraska, Peter B., 1961–

HV8138 .M48   2001
363.2'0973—dc21   2001031228

Designed by Janis Owens

Composed in Sabon by Coghill Composition Company in Richmond, Virginia. Printed and bound by the Maple Press Company in York, Pennsylvania. The paper is Sebago Antique, an acid-free sheet.

MANUFACTURED IN THE UNITED STATES OF AMERICA

05   04   03   02   01   5   4   3   2   1

Contents

Contents

Preface

This book is the culmination of research and thought into what the contributors and I consider a significant development—the increasing reliance on the military model, and in some instances the actual U.S. Armed Forces itself, for framing our nation's crime control thinking, policies, and actions. The central feature of this phenomenon is the blurring of distinctions between criminal justice, criminal justice action, the military, and military action. The blurring of military and police personnel, armory, and ideology was most sensationalistically, and tragically, played out during the Waco fiasco. Not only did the military model dominate the thinking and operations of both the initial and final raids of the Branch Davidian residence, but active-duty military personnel and military equipment played an integral role. Most examples of the influence of the military model on criminal justice are more inconspicuous, however, and at first glance some seem mundane. This book seeks to bring the increasing overlap of the criminal justice system and the military into sharper focus by illuminating both its routine and sensational elements.

Through a collection of revealing and at times discomforting essays, our book attempts to accomplish two key objectives. First, the reader completes this book with a better appreciation of the phenomenon itself—its history, size, nature, and serious implications for our society. Second, the military framework used educates the reader about both the crime control apparatus and the military institution in the post–Cold War era. Put differently, we see this book as a unique and effective tool for better understanding the nature of changes in criminal justice and the military. These readings, therefore, should be a good means for grasping:

- Developments, issues, and policies associated with the criminal justice system
- Current trends in the military
- The significance and nature of the blurring distinction between the police and military
- The changing role of the state in advanced modernity
- The changing nature of militarization in our high-tech, information-based society
- Distinctive dimensions of popular culture as they relate to militarization, technology, punishment, gender, and crime control

My first thanks go to all those contributors who met deadlines, stayed congenial despite my continuous e-mails, and helped give me a sense of collective purpose—Charlie Dunlap, Jonathan Simon, Kevin Haggerty, Richard Ericson, Sue Caulfield, Matthew DeMichele, and Tim Dunn. I would also like to acknowledge the high professionalism and good humor of Bill Frohlich and his staff at Northeastern University Press. Finally, I would like to thank my partner, Shannon Leigh Weer, for her supportive and helpful role over the last several years. My contributions to this book have been improved immensely thanks to her generous and gracious feedback. I must apologize to her, however, for sometimes confusing her insights and ideas with my own.

I

Militarized Crime Control in America

—

The Military–Criminal Justice Blur

An Introduction

Peter B. Kraska

On the one hand, this book is about war, threats to national security, advanced military technology, militarization, and militarism. On the other, it is concerned with the civilian police, controlling crime, and the criminal justice apparatus. Traditionally, few have considered it appropriate to study these two hands as parts of the same body. Consistent with a long-standing tenet of democratic governance, the bureaucracy and functions of the military are meant to be clearly separated from the bureaucracy and functions of the police and criminal justice system. The military handles threats to our nation's security from other nations; the crime control system deals with crime, illegal drugs, and internal disorder. In fact, normally a close alliance between the military and the police is associated with repressive governments.

We are in the midst of a momentous historical change that few people are noticing: the traditional distinctions between military, police, and criminal justice are blurring. This book demonstrates that, although only the most ideologically extreme observers are warning of a fully integrated police/military security force (what Laswell termed the "garrison state"), the military and criminal justice overlap is a legitimate and important sociopolitical trend. Examples of this trend include:

- The emergence of large-scale weapons and personnel transference programs from the military to the police. These are designed to provide the civilian police with military surplus goods such as M-16s, armored personnel carriers, an array of cutting-edge technology, and ex-military soldiers to work as police.
- The use of state National Guard units in both marijuana eradication programs and support assistance to the civilian police departments.
- The advent of an unprecedented cooperative relationship between the military and police on a number of fronts, including technology transfer and development programs, data and information processing for the purpose of enhancing internal security, drug and immigrant interdiction at the borders, programs designed to rebuild other countries' internal security, and cross-training in the area of SWAT, counterterrorist, and counter-civil disturbance exercises.
- A steep growth in special units within both corrections (special response teams) and police (SWAT teams) that are modeled directly after military special operations squads such as the Navy Seals. These correctional and police special operations units are now a routine part of the administration and operations of prisons and police departments.
- A normalization of military-style "boot camps" in the correctional system. The aim is to punish and reform law violators by putting them through a rigid regimen of hard work, reeducation, and rigorous exercise, simulating the traditional military boot camp experience.
- A growing tendency to rely on the military model in formulating crime control rationale and operations. This includes not only the pervasive use of military metaphors and language (war on crime, crime fighting) but also an increasing dependence on ideological themes in military and paramilitary culture.

As a part of documenting and discussing the military/criminal justice blur, this book seeks to accomplish two other related tasks. First, by examining the historical and current interconnections between the military model and the criminal justice system, we can gain a more complete understanding of our ever expanding crime control apparatus and some of its thornier issues. The martial concepts developed throughout this book—war, militarism, militarization—are highly instructive for understanding both past and recent developments of the crime control enterprise. Second, studying the military/police connection also instructs us on important changes in today's U.S. military. Since the demise of the Soviet Union, the U.S. Department of Defense has been forced into, and in some cases has embraced, a new role for itself—a *socially useful* military that operates from a much broader view of their role in civilian society.

Aside from enhancing our understanding of the criminal justice and military institutions, why should the average reader care about these developments? For those readers most interested in answers to the "so what" question, this book will not disappoint. The essays examine thoroughly the myriad consequences of this trend, including, to name just a few:

- What the blur portends for our traditional notions of democracy
- The probable effect of infusing crime control efforts with the ideology of militarism
- The potential for runaway bureaucratic growth as the criminal justice and military complex become more entangled
- The potential for more "efficient," technologically advanced, and invasive crime-fighting capabilities
- The dangers of a more internally focused military institution
- The multitude of ways in which this trend could infringe on citizens' civil rights and violate human rights

In sum, this book provides an examination and assessment of the military/criminal justice blur. It is also designed to be a learning tool. Through the development of a unique set of conceptual lenses, we seek to render a more complete and current understanding of our criminal justice system and the public policies governing it. It also illuminates the changing nature of the U.S. military and its influence on civilian society.

A Research Journey into the Land of SWAT

In 1989 a friend asked me to join him on a U.S. Coast Guard exercise. I went along only out of friendship and curiosity; little did I know that eleven years later I would still be studying that outing's implications. As we patrolled the shores of Lake Erie, I learned from a Coast Guard officer that the U.S. Navy routinely used a team of five to eight Coast Guard personnel on their drug-interdiction training exercises off the coast of Florida. When the navy ship stopped a suspicious vessel, it was the Coast Guard personnel who had the law enforcement powers to search, seize, and arrest. He admitted readily that this was designed to circumvent the navy policies against being involved in civilian police actions.

Soon thereafter, I found U.S. congressional hearing documents that detailed how politicians had been quietly debating the role of the U.S. military in the enforcement of drug laws since 1980. Ronald Reagan resurrected the war against drugs immediately after his first election; a key component of his "new" drug war was to enlist the help of the U.S. Armed Forces. Reagan, along with congressional drug war enthusiasts, pushed hard for the repeal of the Posse Comitatus Act of 1878, which delineates in law the clear separation between internal law enforcement conducted by civilian police and external security functions carried out by the military. This mainstay of Western democracy was being called into question with little recognition from academics or the public (see chapter 3 for more on the fate of the Posse Comitatus Act). I researched what I later titled the "military as drug cops" phenomenon from 1989 to 1993.[1]

I did not realize that another significant trend was already underway that provided the rest of the militarization story. Again, based on an invitation from an acquaintance, I entered the real world of bureaucratic change and began conducting an ethnography on the formation of small-town SWAT teams (see chapter 9). I ended up spending the latter third of the 1990s researching another almost completely overlooked development in the U.S. police institution—the militarization of a component of the civilian police. A two-year-long ethnography and two independently funded national surveys of police departments documented some important changes in the military model's influence on civilian policing.

This research garnered a good deal of print and television media coverage from 1997 through the early part of 2000. It might never have been noticed outside the halls of academe if it were not for William Booth from the *Washington Post,* who listened to an academic radio show that mentioned my study. Two weeks later he wrote a front-page lead story titled "Exploding Number of SWAT Teams Sets Off Alarms: Critics See Growing Role of Heavily Armed Police Units as 'Militarization' of Law Enforcement." Since then I have participated in putting together and providing interviews for at least sixty stories carried by various news media, including the "Jim Lehrer News Hour," the *New York Times,* the *Los Angeles Times,* the *Economist,* National Public Radio, the *Boston Globe,* the "CBS Evening News," Peter Jennings's "World News Tonight," and a Discovery Channel documentary.[2]

This research on U.S. paramilitary policing has been an integral part of my journey in understanding the military model's influence on the police and contemporary crime control. It contradicts, however, other police scholarship, which claims that the police institution is entering a new era: a shift away from the paramilitary, professional model of policing promoted between 1950 and 1980 to a democratized model known as "community policing."[3] As opposed to the community policing literature, where there is no definitive answer as to whether this is a change in rhetoric or substance, two national-level surveys have documented over time the recent and certain militarization of a component of the police institution.[4]

This militarization is reflected by a precipitous rise and the widespread mainstreaming of police paramilitary units (PPUs). These police units, referred to most often as special weapons and tactics (SWAT) teams or special response teams, are tailored after military special operations groups such as the Navy Seals. Until recently, these units were only a peripheral part of larger police departments reacting to the rare hostage, barricaded suspect, or civil disturbance incident.

As of the end of 1995, 89 percent of American police departments serving populations of fifty thousand or more had a PPU, almost double of what existed in 1980.[5] Their growth in smaller jurisdictions (twenty-five thousand to fifty thousand people) has been even more pronounced. We have seen a 157 percent increase in the number of units between 1985 and 1995. As of the end of 1995, over 65 percent of small-town departments had a PPU; today there are almost eighteen police officers serving on a PPU per one hundred officers in these smaller jurisdictions (most are part-time assignments where the remainder of their time is spent doing routine patrol work). If we combine data from large and small departments, we see that the paramilitary unit approach is becoming an integral part of contemporary policing in all departments serving localities with twenty-five thousand or more people. In 1995 over 77 percent of police departments had a paramilitary unit, an increase of almost 48 percent since 1985. Police reported 29,962 paramilitary deployments in 1995, a 939 percent increase over the 2,884 call-outs of 1980. Over 20 percent of all departments with PPUs use the units for "proactive patrol work" (patrolling high-crime areas in teams of four to twelve officers targeting suspicious vehicles and citizens), a 257 percent increase since the beginning of 1989.[6]

The U.S. military is providing an unprecedented amount of training and weaponry to the police. Earlier research found that almost half of the PPUs surveyed had trained with active-duty military special operations experts. Numerous departments admitted their close involvement with the Navy Seals and the Army Rangers.[7]

The bulk of the deployments that paramilitary units engage in today are for the execution of no-knock warrants.[8] In both large and small departments, PPUs routinely carry out dangerous contraband raids on people's private residences, often in the predawn hours, for purposes of conducting a crude form of investigation into drug and gun law violations.

Using SWAT teams for proactive patrol work has also become popular. This is where police paramilitary officers patrol the streets as a team, often dressed in full BDUs (battle-dress uniforms) and carrying automatic weaponry, targeting "disorderly" areas for the purpose of restoring "a climate of order." This is obviously a dramatic departure from the standard-fare cop on the beat reacting to calls for service. Paramilitary units aggressively occupying "hot spots"—areas identified as high-crime sectors by sophisticated computer mapping programs—for the purpose of proactively restoring order, through the incursion of pedestrians, loiterers, suspicious automobiles, and suspicious residences, resonates with police tactics in Northern Ireland.[9] Both proactive PPU patrol and PPU contraband raids are touted in most departments as consistent with community policing reforms in that they are targeting "community disorder" (see chapter 6).

Police paramilitary units are also on the cutting edge of using advanced military technology. These units employ the latest in military garb, weaponry, surveillance equipment, an array of "less-than-lethal" use-of-force devices, body armor, listening devices, and communications equipment. An enormous for-profit industry promotes heavily the hardware associated with PPUs by playing on the imagery of the military special operations soldier in their advertisements (see chapter 9 for more on police paramilitary subculture). In addition, the Department of Defense has donated a massive amount of military surplus to police paramilitary units over the last five years. The most common items are armored personnel carriers, M-16s, and night vision devices (see chapter 4 for more on this practice).

An Overview of Each Chapter

I discovered during the course of my research that I was not alone. Other academics, journalists, and practitioners had noticed and were beginning to write about related trends. This book is where our journeys intersect. The nine essays in this volume constitute the first concerted effort at documenting and discussing the broader agenda of examining the influence that war, militarism, and militarization have had and are increasingly having on the thinking and operations associated with the crime control enterprise. Each of the essays focuses on a different dimension of this general theme.

The following chapter, "Crime Control as Warfare: Language Matters," develops the organizing concepts used throughout this book and examines the powerful role that the language of war and the military model has on our society's handling of crime. It makes the concepts "militarism" and "militarization" relevant to today's society and provides seven key features of what I call "high-modern militarization." It also establishes the inward turn of the war/military paradigm in U.S. society, arguing that internal difficulties such as crime and drugs have become in some ways our new Cold War. The chapter provides a poignant example of this shift by examining the attempt by some military analysts to reconstruct the crime problem as one of "insurgency" requiring a "counterinsurgency" approach, using the new military doctrine of limited warfare known as "low-intensity conflict."

The four essays that make up part 2, "The Military-Police Blur," examine different aspects of the fading distinctions between the military and the police. The first piece is written by a nationally recognized military practitioner who has, in a series of influential essays, raised and analyzed tough questions about the U.S. military's changing role in the post–Cold War era. In "The Thick Green Line" Colonel Charles Dunlap provides an engaging historical overview of the delineation between military and police services and the rapid erosion of this tradition. He discusses the likely role that domestic terrorism and computer crime will have on this trend, updating our understanding of the probable direction, pervasiveness, and consequences of the military's increasing involvement in domestic law enforcement. Colonel Dunlap elucidates the practical and philosophical stakes in allowing the military mission to creep into civilian police functions.

Chapter 4, written by Kevin Haggerty and Richard Ericson, provides a fascinating look at the militarization of the civilian police not through a turn toward coercive force but rather through an emerging relationship between the military's techno-science capabilities, its associated high-technology and information industries, and the criminal justice system. The authors document in detail the shift the military-industrial complex has made toward the internal problems of crime and criminal justice as an important part of their legitimacy. They also diagram a helpful visual model showing exactly how the military and its technology/information capabilities are influencing the police in the post–Cold War era. It would be hard to complete this chapter and not have a keen appreciation of, and possibly a new uneasiness about, how the criminal justice and the military complexes are converging in previously unthought-of ways in the areas of communications, information, and surveillance technology.

Timothy Dunn provides a path-breaking examination of the militarization of the U.S.-Mexico border by focusing specifically on the military's direct involvement in drug and immigration enforcement. His essay provides us with a rich analysis of the coalescing of police and military bureaucracies, and it makes clear the human rights difficulties contained within this approach. His exhibition of a "spectrum" or continuum of militarization is quite helpful in conceptualizing this phenomenon as one of degrees.

The final chapter in part 2 makes sense of the simultaneous rise of reform efforts aimed at democratizing police services (community policing) and reforms that indicate a more aggressive approach based on the military model. This essay familiarizes the reader with the community policing literature, paramilitary policing trends, and a new way of understanding criminal justice trends and practices—referred to as a "governmentality" framework. Matthew DeMichele and Peter Kraska conclude that the emergence of these seemingly incoherent macrostrategies does not necessarily signal a floundering and ambivalent state in crisis. To the contrary, in the real world of application, they actually exhibit a type of "strategic coherence." The numerous ramifications of this counterintuitive conclusion are explored.

These four essays in part 2 establish the pervasiveness and importance of the military-police blur as a legitimate trend. They also demonstrate the rapidly changing nature of state control and point to what we can likely expect in the future with regard to the importance of the military model's role in criminal justice operations, the central place of technology and information, and the emergence of an overlaying of both overt coercive controls and more subtle high-modern controls.

The essays in part 3, "Militarism Comes Home," broaden the discussion into the areas of punishment, feminism, and popular culture. In chapter 7 Jonathan Simon presents an intriguing analysis of the past and current role of the military model on the areas of punishment and corrections. He examines how since the Vietnam War traditional militarism has been replaced with a "new war culture," which has direct connections into the paradigm our country has adopted in "fighting" the enemy of crime and drugs. Simon describes how this new paramilitary culture provides a powerful narrative for recent martial trends in corrections, including the normalization of special response teams (the correctional equivalent of SWAT teams), the increasingly popular Supermax prisons, and drug war boot camps. He also explores the role the military has played in the development of cyborgism and systems analysis, demonstrating convincingly their link to the aforementioned developments.

Susan Caulfield, in chapter 8, also examines correctional boot camps, but within a context that analyzes from a feminist perspective both the relationship between militarism and feminism and the central role militarism plays in our handling of crime. She shows how revenge, solving problems through violence, and glorifying the tools of violence are all central features of the reciprocation between both crime commission and crime fighting. Her feminist gaze illuminates the social arrangements that emanate from militarist ideology and provides thought-provoking alternatives that revolve around the notion of "transformative justice." The reader can learn a great deal about not only the nature and definition of militarism but also the clarity with which feminist lenses can aid in our understanding of violence in America.

Chapter 9, "Playing War: Masculinity, Militarism, and Their Real-World Consequences," presents a description and analysis of my firsthand experience with militarized culture during a two-year-long "in the trenches" ethnography of rural police officers and military soldiers working together to form SWAT teams. The military subculture uncovered in this research is related to common features of popular culture. The conclusion links the Oklahoma City bombing and Waco incidents as expressions of the same long-standing cultural pattern.

Controlling the Citizenry: A Few Implications

This book is a starting point for acknowledging and exploring the role war, the military, and the military model have on crime and drug control efforts in the post–Cold War era. The objective is to begin to untangle and make sense of a labyrinth of cultural, political, and material links between the U.S. military-industrial complex, processes of militarization, and the crime and drug control apparatus. Our broader purpose is to explore the implications of this trend in order to understand changes in the nature of social control.

We have witnessed in only the last fifteen years a significant departure from the strong tradition in the United States of eschewing the military as a model for civilian police. This book should demonstrate to readers that a central feature of our government is fading: the clear delineation in form and function between internal security forces (civilian police) and external security forces (the military). This transformation signals a historic shift in the nature of the state, how it secures (or attempts to secure) compliance, and the overall character of modern social control.

Of course, this shift may be more accurately seen as a recent and rapid acceleration of a long-term trend of militarism and militarization creeping into civilian governmental functions. Falling back on the military model for handling difficult internal social problems is logically consistent with the criminal justice enterprise's increasing reliance on the use of force, rationality, technology, and information collection and processing. It should not be surprising, therefore, that the military-industrial complex and the criminal justice enterprise, in sharing so many ideological and material features, including a common government, would in the post–Cold War era share data, cross-train, engage in joint exercises, share weaponry, and borrow from each other's expertise.

From a bureaucracy-building perspective, both players benefit in this scenario. The military is able to broaden its mandate in the post–Cold War era from large-scale wars protecting our sovereignty to a host of internal social problems. The criminal justice enterprise gains by tapping into the advanced technology and large budget of the military complex, as well as by shrouding itself in the assumed competence, efficiency, and effectiveness of the military model. Being more military-like lends a perceived legitimacy and professionalism to crime control efforts.

Where these changes will lead is impossible to predict. For some analysts on the far left and far right these trends might portend the rise of Laswell's "garrison state," or an emerging police state, or possibly a new form of totalitarianism. Others will view it merely as a rational outgrowth of an evolving high-modern society where structural distinctions such as private/public and police/military have diminished meaning and function. Whatever the case, it is important to avoid viewing these developments as the state merely resorting to raw force. Instead, the militarization of the criminal justice enterprise represents not a regression toward crude tactics but an advancement in bureaucratic surveillance and sophistication that coincides with other advanced changes in our high-modern society.

It would be a mistake, however, to allow the pervasiveness of high-modern controls to blind us to the ever present strong arm of the state. As demonstrated so vividly in the Waco disaster, and in the tens of thousands of no-knock contraband raids carried out by police paramilitary units per year, the state is integrating its prerogative to use overt violence with its developing abilities to gain compliance through more sophisticated means.

Notes

1. See Peter B. Kraska, "Militarizing the Drug War: A Sign of the Times," in *Altered States of Mind: Critical Observations of the Drug War,* ed. Peter B. Kraska (New York: Garland, 1993).
2. What exactly all of this media attention actually accomplished is not quite clear. It resulted in no fame, no money, and no appreciable difference in the phenomenon itself. For examples of the type of coverage see M. Arax, "Small Town's SWAT Team Leaves Costly Legacy," *Los Angeles Times,* 5 April 1999, A1, A9; P. Bass, "Neighborhood Warriors: Thanks

to the Drug War, SWAT Teams Sweep into Small Communities," *New Haven Advocate,* 18 December 1997, 14–22; D. Manasian, "The Sultans of SWAT," *Economist,* 2 October 1999, 60–65; T. Egan, "Soldiers of the Drug War Remain on Duty," *New York Times,* 1 March 1999, A1, A16; W. Booth, "Exploding Number of SWAT Teams Sets Off Alarms," *Washington Post,* 17 June 1997, 1–3.

3. See Edward Maguire, "Structural Changes in Large Municipal Police Organizations during the Community Policing Era," *Justice Quarterly* 14 (1997): 547–76.

4. See Peter B. Kraska and Victor E. Kappeler, "Militarizing American Police: The Rise and Normalization of Paramilitary Units," *Social Problems* 44 (1997): 1–18; Peter B. Kraska and Louis J. Cubellis, "Militarizing Mayberry and Beyond: Making Sense of American Paramilitary Policing," *Justice Quarterly* 14 (1997): 607–29.

5. Kraska and Kappeler, "Militarizing American Police."

6. Kraska and Cubellis, "Militarizing Mayberry."

7. Kraska and Kappeler, "Militarizing American Police"; Kraska and Cubellis, "Militarizing Mayberry."

8. Kraska and Kappeler, "Militarizing American Police"; Kraska and Cubellis, "Militarizing Mayberry."

9. Malcolm Feeley and Jonathan Simon, "Actuarial Justice: The Emerging New Criminal Law," in *The Futures of Criminology,* ed. D. Nelken (Beverly Hills: Sage, 1994), 173–201.

2

Crime Control as Warfare

Language Matters

Peter B. Kraska

The military model is as pervasive as the medical model in efforts to colonize the control of crime and other forms of deviance.

Richard Ericson, criminologist, 1994

Someone steals a bike; another sells a hot gun to a delinquent; someone else bashes the head of a rival into a car door; another kills his ex-wife after stalking her for months; and yet another ignores safety regulations at a factory, resulting in an employee's death. There can be no doubt that crime is a problem. It is also a problem easily exaggerated, but even if it is not that bad statistically, most Americans still want a concerted reaction. How do we organize our response? Ericson's quotation above observes that we have relied heavily on military ideology and practice, yet this fact has been almost completely ignored by crime and justice academics.

If the language we use to characterize our response to law breaking is any indication, this is a serious oversight. We fight crime, conduct a war on crime and a war on drugs, crack down, raid private residences for contraband, conduct street sweeps, have zero tolerance for law breakers, detain people in boot camps, and even execute the enemy (death penalty). Is this language mere media-driven rhetoric meant only in a figurative sense?

The language we use to frame our solutions to the crime problem matters. Martial language—while not necessarily being the cause of an aggressive, militarized reaction—can intensify society's response. Moreover, and most importantly, the language we employ serves as a good indicator of the values and beliefs we use to structure our crime control actions and policies. The purpose of this chapter, therefore, is to examine the role of militaristic language in crime control efforts and provide a much needed update on the two central organizing concepts used throughout this book—militarization and militarism. Highlights of the chapter include the development of the concept "high-modern militarization," the role of the war metaphor in crime campaigns in U.S. history, and an example of the power of language through examining military analysts' reframing of the crime problem as one of "insurgency" requiring "counterinsurgency" measures.

Conceptual Clarification: High-Modern Militarization

Traditionally, war has been conceived of as state-sanctioned armies attempting to take over each other's territories using lethal violence. *Militarization* was merely the preparation for this activity. *Militarism* is a cultural pattern of beliefs and values supporting war and militarization that comes to dominate a society (e.g., Nazi Germany).[1] These early conceptions and their brutish connotations help explain why sociology, despite the central place war and militarization have played throughout U.S. history, has traditionally eschewed them in theorizing society. They refer to crude, highly violent, and antiquated state activity better left to war historians and political scientists.[2] With contemporary theories of social control emphasizing a decline in state physical violence and an ascendance of softer controls—those rooted in mundane regulations, ideology, and surveillance controls, for example—resurrecting organizing concepts such as "militarization" may even seem misplaced in this "high-modern" society. However, scholars have begun to develop a more current and nuanced understanding of martial concepts and an appreciation for the central role these phenomena play in the makeup of contemporary society.[3]

Indeed, it is the lack of attention paid to the influence of the military and the military model that has left organizing concepts such as "militarism" and "militarization" undeveloped, even though their influence thrives. Just as the medical field and the criminal law institution have transformed strikingly as they have modernized, so has militarism and the processes of militarization, particularly since the advent of nuclear weapons, and now in the post–Cold War era. The nature of the state's use of violence and the maintenance of its security have not avoided the same high-modern developments in our medical or legal systems. Indeed, much of what we consider to be "high-modern" has its origins in the military complex.

An antecedent to examining the militarization of criminal justice, therefore, is the updating of traditional martial concepts. *Militarization,* for instance, can be defined in its broadest terms as the social process in which society organizes itself for the production of violence or the threat thereof. As chapter 4 so convincingly demonstrates, technology and information have become a central aspect, if not the predominant feature, of this production process. Militarism is merely militarization's supporting ideology. It is a set of beliefs and values that stress the use of force and domination as appropriate means to solve problems and gain political power. It glorifies military power, hardware, and technology as its primary problem-solving tools.

What we think of as traditional "war" is less relevant in today's militarization. In the scramble to define a new post–Cold War mission, "security specialists"—an amalgam of military think-tank analysts, defense industry experts, military academicians, and Pentagon officials—have given up on the "communist threat" as their basis of legitimacy. In its place they have constructed a new narrative justifying the military's preeminence relying not on the notion of war but rather on such terms as "low-intensity conflict" (LIC), "operations other than war" (OOTW), and the "gray area phenomenon" (GAP).

LIC, OOTW, and GAP refer to internal difficulties facing governments not readily solvable by traditional war but still supposedly requiring some sort of military response. Examples abound in a rapidly changing geopolitical environment: terrorism, nongovernmental paramilitary forces, information systems security, famine, environmental destruction, civil unrest, ethnic cleansing, immigration problems, and natural disaster relief. An important development, therefore, in our high-modern society, is the reframing of certain social problems as amenable to direct military intervention.

Tangible indices of this sort of high-modern militarization and militarism are found throughout this book. A summary would include:

1. A blurring of external and internal security functions leading to a targeting of civilian populations, internal "security" threats, and a focus on aggregate populations as potential internal "insurgents"

16

2. An avoidance of overt or lethal violence, with a greater emphasis placed on information gathering and processing, surveillance work, and less-than-lethal technologies
3. An ideology and theoretical framework of militarism that stresses that effective problem solving requires state force, technology, armament, intelligence gathering, aggressive suppression efforts, and other assorted activities commensurate with modern military thinking and operations
4. Criminal justice practices guided by the ideological framework of militarism, such as the use of special-operations paramilitary teams in policing and corrections, policing activities that emphasize military tactics such as drug, gun, and gang suppression, and punishment models based on the military boot camp
5. The purchasing, loaning, donation, and use of actual material products that can be characterized as militaristic, including a range of military armaments, transportation devices, surveillance equipment, and military-style garb
6. A rapidly developing collaboration, at the highest level of the governmental and corporate worlds, between the defense industry and the crime control industry
7. The use of military language within political and popular culture to characterize the social problems of drugs, crime, and social disorder

Post–Cold War Developments Highlight Neglect

Richard Quinney pointed to the influence of militarism and prevalence of militarization as early as 1974. He made sense of the explosive growth of the crime control enterprise during the days of the Law Enforcement Assistance Administration (LEAA) using martial concepts like those outlined above. Noting parallels between the complex of interests and beneficiaries associated with the military industrial complex (MIC) and the burgeoning criminal justice system, Quinney named the conglomerate the "criminal-justice-industrial complex" (CJIC). A key point made by Quinney, which no subsequent scholarship has elaborated on, was that the MIC and CJIC not only were following parallel courses but were also ideological compatriots that were beginning to cross-fertilize materially.[4]

Except for this early effort, criminologists have neglected the deep influence the war/military paradigm has had and continues to have on state crime control thinking, organization, and activities. This is understandable considering the neglect of sociologists in examining the important role war, militarism, and militarization have played in the development of society and the state.[5]

Trends in U.S. society, as embodied in the often heard question "Is fighting crime and drugs our new Cold War?," are beginning to illuminate this neglect. Indeed, it is hard to avoid the connection between the resurgence in "battling" crime and drugs and what should be viewed as a watershed event in crime control history, the end of the Cold War:

> With the cold war brought to an end, in a situation with deep economic recession, and where the most important industrial nations have no external enemies to mobilize against, it seems not improbable that the war against inner enemies will receive top priority according to well-established historical precedents.[6]

Numerous scholars have observed that the recent escalation of the war on crime and drugs is associated with the loss of an ideological centerpiece in U.S. society—the enemy of communism. Nadelman views changes associated with the post–Cold War era as central in understanding shifts in crime control: "Where once anti-communism represented the principal moral imperative of U.S. foreign policy, drug enforcement and other criminal justice objectives have emerged as the new moral imperatives."[7]

In an exhaustive historical examination of the impact of war and militarization on U.S. society, Sherry demonstrates how throughout American history the U.S. government has demonized and rallied against common enemies with military force or the threat thereof.[8] At the root of this tendency are varying interests and motivations, including the construction of a national purpose and unity, the growth of governmental and industrial complexes, and the advancement of state power by allowing for extreme measures to be taken in order to "fight" the feared enemy. The difference in today's sociopolitical environment is that the line between waging actual war against external enemies and metaphorical wars waged against internal enemies is becoming increasingly blurred:

> The war on drugs was becoming a ubiquitous metaphor, used by the media, politicians, and citizens in everyday talk and elaborated floridly in references to "battle plans," "fronts," and "enemies." . . . Americans were finding "wars" to wage all over their political and cultural agenda. As they did so, they marked the completion of the inward turn of militarization.[9]

Internalizing militarization is marked not only by political and media rhetoric but also by the acquiescence of the armed forces themselves to admonishments by politicians to make themselves more "socially useful"—the most persuasive example being the military's extensive involvement in drug law enforcement (see chapter 3). Equally important is the distinct possibility that state crime and drug control efforts are drawing heavily from military ideology, tactics, organization, and hardware (i.e., the militarization of criminal justice).

Politics and Warfare: Militarized Language and Its Consequences

Language and metaphors play a powerful role in the construction of reality: they clarify values and understanding and guide problem-solving processes. Filtering the crime and drug problems through militaristic metaphors thus will likely result in thoughts and actions that correspond with the war/military paradigm. As mentioned earlier, the pervasive use of militaristic discourse in U.S. society to address social problems is one indication of an incremental inward turn of militarization.

Martial crime-control rhetoric, so ubiquitous in contemporary political and media culture, originated out of post–World War II politicians employing the "war" metaphor as a means to rally public support for addressing various social ills. President Lyndon Johnson in 1966 was the first presidential politician to call for a "war on crime," along with wars on disease, poverty, "the inhumanity of man," and hunger—in an attempt to divert attention away from the escalating conflict in Vietnam.[10] President Richard Nixon followed Johnson's and Barry Goldwater's lead by ratcheting up the intensity of "war" discourse in his draconian campaign against heroin users and low-level distributors. He labeled drug abuse as "public enemy number one," equating the problem with "foreign troops on our shores."[11]

The Reagan, Bush, and Clinton presidential administrations, along with the mainstream media, have further militarized crime control discourse by radiating the master metaphor of "war" into a flood of taken-for-granted martial expressions and submetaphors. Ronald Reagan praised police chiefs "who command the front lines in America's battle for public order" and "the thin blue line that holds back a jungle which threatens to reclaim the clearing we call civilization."[12] Reagan routinely equated the evils of communism with the threat of drugs and crime. He even went as far as codifying war talk into law by declaring, through presidential directive, "drugs" as an official threat to national security.[13]

President George Bush and Congress during the late 1980s engaged in a game of political "one-upmanship" when battling over who could sound the most bellicose in the "war" on drugs and crime, blanketing political and media discourse with talk about "front lines," "battlefields," "drug work camps," "drug war bonds," "drug czars," and "calling out the troops." It became common for politicians during the apex of the drug war to characterize U.S. society as a "nation under siege":

> There is no greater threat to the survival of our society than drugs. If the present condition continues, we will no longer be free, independent citizens but people entwined and imprisoned by drugs. The military forces of this country must become more involved.[14]

The Clinton administration directed its martial rhetoric less on the threat of drugs and more on urban and gun violence (i.e., the "war on violence"). Drug war discourse has still taken front stage, however, when politically expedient. Consider Bill Clinton's comments during the appointment ceremony of Army General Barry McCaffrey to the civilian position of "drug czar":

> McCaffrey has faced down many threats to America's national security, from guerrilla warfare in the jungles of Vietnam to the unprecedented ground war in the sands of Desert Storm. Now he faces a more insidious but no less formidable enemy in illegal drugs.[15]

As this quotation demonstrates, martial rhetoric directed at crime and drugs has serious real-world consequences. What is at stake for politicians and bureaucrats who frame the crime problem in martial terms is the legitimacy and security of the state itself. The above quotations insinuate that we risk our "national security" by *not* waging war. This type of language invokes those state agencies with the power to use state-sanctioned violence. The military and criminal justice systems have the capability to handle the drug/crime problem as a type of "insurrection," justifying a militaristic response, including campaigns to occupy, control, and restore state-defined order to public and private space, as well as operating detention facilities designed to punish and warehouse the prisoners of this "war" (see the discussions of correctional "boot camps" in chapters 7 and 8).

Language in Action: The Case of the Military as Police

The intensification of drug and crime war discourse comes at a time when the largest military-industrial complex in the world is losing its forty-year-long justification for its existence and growth. As might be expected, the state has resisted diminishing the size and power of its symbol of international superiority. As mentioned earlier, one tactic has been to modify the military's mandate to include a more active role in "helping out" U.S. society on a number of new domestic battle fronts.

Given that this is such a dramatic shift in the armed forces' focus, one might expect a vigorous national debate. After all, the U.S. Constitution and Bill of Rights were formed in large part out of a fear of military power and rule. Tight civilian control over the armed forces, intended to minimize their direct influence on internal affairs, is still a central indicator of democratic governance around the world. What follows therefore is a brief discussion of a potentially momentous yet peculiarly silent shift in the nature of the military/police-security apparatus.

The United States has developed a strong tradition, as found in legislation and administrative policies, that clearly demarcates military and police forces and their activities—the most well-known policy statement being the Posse Comitatus Act of 1878. Posse Comitatus had enforced a relatively strict delineation between military and police activity until the Reagan administration worked for its repeal in 1981 as part of their plan to launch a new drug war. Over the next fifteen years, as the drug war increased in intensity, three presidents and Congress whittled away at the act and its intent through numerous amendments and official directives. As a result, all branches of the military now engage in fully cooperative arrangements and operations with civilian police, the only restriction being that soldiers cannot take the lead in arresting or searching U.S. citizens. Pentagon officials initially resisted this shift, viewing it as a devolution of their function, that is, until they recognized the fiduciary advantages of becoming more "socially useful" in the post–Cold War era.

Earlier I discussed the shift among security analysts away from traditional notions of "war" and toward new models of military conflict using concepts such as "low-intensity conflict" (LIC). Timothy Dunn, in his book *The Militarization of the U.S.-Mexico Border,* provides a compelling case study of politicians and the new military reconstituting the problems of drugs and illegal immigration at the U.S.-Mexico border as "national security threats." Emphasizing the shift in focus to "internal defense," he defines the doctrine of low-intensity conflict as

> the establishment and maintenance of social control over targeted civilian populations through the implementation of a broad range of sophis-

ticated measures via the coordinated and integrated efforts of police, paramilitary, and military forces. One of the doctrine's distinguishing characteristics is that military forces take on police functions, while police forces take on military characteristics. In theory, low-intensity conflict is a comparatively subtle form of militarization.[16]

The most ideologically compatible and thus most popular battle front for the new military has been social problems amenable to actual security strategies and tactics, such as urban violence, illegal drugs, and illegal immigration. Not surprisingly, these new military targets are touted by security specialists as emerging trends necessitating the military's involvement. Clearly these problems existed previous to the end of the Cold War; hence, what we have are not problems in search of a solution but a solution in search of problems.

Klare calls the military's encroachment into civilian affairs the *national security syndrome:* "the tendency to expand the definition of national security to require ever-greater control over national life."[17] The impetus for this syndrome stems from the construction of certain internal difficulties as so "threatening" that the only option left is resorting to military power. Colonel Dunlap interprets this development in the post–Cold War environment as a type of "postmodern militarism," characterized by

a growing willingness of an increasingly militarily-naive society to charge those in uniform with responsibilities that a democracy ought to leave to civilians. It is a product of America's deep frustration and disgust with elected government's inability to work effectively, or to even labor honestly. . . . Embattled politicians are ever more frequently turning to the military for quick-fixes: Can't stop drugs? Call in the Navy. FEMA overwhelmed? Deploy the Airborne. Crime out of control? Put Guardsmen on the streets. Troubled youths? Marine role models and military boot camps.[18]

Moreover, within the ranks of military officials, epitomized in a political figure such as General Colin Powell, is a growing "neopraetorian culture," defined as a desire to refashion a deteriorating society in the image of military society (e.g., orderly, disciplined, efficient, respectful). Neopraetorianism arises when the armed forces perceive themselves not only as protectors of what is right in civil society but also as the self-appointed and, importantly, unelected makers and implementers of the same. "Neopraetorianism is marked by the military's flawed notion of its own cultural superiority and its seeming inability to grasp the merits of civil society."[19]

From "postmodern militarism," the military's "neopraetorianism," and a rudderless military establishment has arisen an incremental reframing of law breaking as a "social threat" justifying the employment of the armed forces. The language used in LIC, GAP, and OOTW is designed in part to reconceptualize law breaking and social disorder as "national security" issues. In a peculiar application of what has normally been a leftist interpretation of crime, security specialists promoting these doctrines are *politicizing* crime and social disorder by redefining them as a type of insurgency, so as to legitimate a "counterinsurgency" approach.

Turbiville, a security specialist in "low-intensity conflict," cites illegal immigration, urban gangs, the illegal drug trade, and organized crime as appropriate targets for military intervention under the LIC doctrine. One author in a book edited by Turbiville compares the civil unrest found in Northern Ireland with the "combat-like" conditions of urban America.

> Crime in America is not thought of by most as "political"—in particular, it has not been directed towards terrorist intimidation of the populace, though it may certainly have that effect. More important, as we have noted repeatedly, it is localized as it is in Northern Ireland or any other insurgent-affected area. What we have, then, are human cesspools—in every sense already centers of criminal activity, as well as economic and spiritual poverty, well beyond anything Northern Ireland can throw up in terms of misery and death—waiting for some jolt to create waves that leap out of the pool.[20]

The author concludes that the military/police security apparatus in the United States has far more justification than even Northern Ireland officials for invoking the LIC/counterinsurgency doctrine. He critiques current police efforts and suggests the Northern Ireland approach:

> Police are relatively ineffective in dealing with hard-hit areas, of course, because they violate the most elementary rules of counterinsurgency. They do not systematically seize and clear areas, leaving behind "militia." Rather, they chase the guerrilla "main forces" over hill and dale. They do not see the problem from this perspective, though, and so do not utilize procedures that are routine in areas as diverse as Sri Lanka or Northern Ireland.[21]

The author reports hope, however, in noting changing police tactics where the police have adopted a "counterinsurgency," low-intensity conflict model. He sees certain cutting-edge police tactics such as "street sweeps," "no-knock contraband raids," "weed and seed" programs, and "quality-of-life enforcement" as consistent with the LIC doctrine. All of these police tactics emphasize the occupation of territory with overwhelming manpower, the suppression of crime and disorder through force, and then a restoration of that same territory.[22]

These aforementioned changes in language are not isolated to military think-tank circles. In the most widely read police-practitioner magazine in the world, another "security specialist" frames the "gang problem" as a phenomenon in need of a militarized approach:

> Street gangs will likely represent a fundamental threat to U.S. security in the future. To respond to this potential threat, law enforcement officials and scholars must begin to establish closer ties to their counterparts in military and national security studies. We must create a coordinated watch on street gang genesis to ensure that this new form of soldier is not allowed to emerge in our neighborhoods.[23]

Conclusion: Language Matters

Of course, the discourse of analysts does not indicate a coming totalitarianism via the war on crime. What it does demonstrate, though, is the power of language. The war metaphor, more than just a cliché, reflects the ideological underpinnings of post–Cold War crime control efforts. Metaphors mirror the values we harbor. The tendency of our society to adopt the values embodied in the military model to solve internal problems such as crime and drugs signals the degree to which the tenets of high-modern militarism are institutionalized in our civilian affairs, our government, and our culture. As the next four chapters demonstrate, the real-world manifestations of this ideological framework are dauntingly real. These chapters also illustrate, however, that this is an advanced form of militarization, one that would not be readily obvious to those that faced Nazi Germany.

Notes

1. A. Vagts, *A History of Militarism: Civilian and Military* (New York: Free Press, 1959); J. Donovan, *Militarism, U.S.A* (New York: Scribner, 1970).
2. C. Dandeker, *Surveillance, Power, and Modernity: Bureaucracy and Discipline from 1700 to the Present Day* (New York: St. Martin's, 1990); A. Giddens, *The Nation-State and Violence* (Cambridge: Polity Press, 1985); M. Sherry, *In the Shadow of War: The United States since the 1930s* (New Haven: Yale University Press, 1995).

3. See M. Mann, *The Sources of Social Power,* vol. 1 (Cambridge: Cambridge University Press, 1986); Dandeker, *Surveillance, Power, and Modernity;* Giddens, *The Nation-State and Violence;* Sherry, *In the Shadow of War.*
4. R. Quinney, *Critique of Legal Order: Crime Control in Capitalist Society* (Boston: Little, Brown, 1974); P. B. Kraska, "Militarizing the Drug War: A Sign of the Times," in *Altered States of Mind: Critical Observations of the Drug War,* ed. P. B. Kraska (New York: Garland, 1993), 159–206; P. B. Kraska, "The Police and Military in the Post–Cold War Era: Streamlining the State's Use of Force Entities in the Drug War," *Police Forum* 4 (1994): 1–8.
5. Mann, *The Sources of Social Power;* Giddens, *The Nation-State and Violence.*
6. N. Christie, *Crime Control as Industry: Towards Gulags, Western Style* (New York: Routledge, 1994), 16.
7. E. A. Nadelman, *Cops across Borders: The Internationalization of U.S. Criminal Law Enforcement* (University Park: Pennsylvania State University Press, 1993), 475.
8. Sherry, *In the Shadow of War.*
9. Sherry, *In the Shadow of War,* 431.
10. Sherry, *In the Shadow of War.*
11. V. E. Kappeler and G. Potter, *The Mythology of Crime and Criminal Justice* (Prospect Heights, Ill.: Waveland, 1996).
12. Sherry, *In the Shadow of War,* 445.
13. Kraska, *Altered States of Mind.*
14. Committee on the Armed Services, *Narcotics Interdiction and the Use of the Military: Issues for Congress* (Washington, D.C.: U.S. Government Printing Office, 1988).
15. Kappeler and Potter, *Mythology of Crime,* 95.
16. T. J. Dunn, *The Militarization of the U.S.-Mexico Border: Low-Intensity Doctrine Comes Home* (Austin: University of Texas Press, 1996), 4.
17. M. Klare, "Militarism: The Issues Today," in *Problems of Contemporary Militarism,* ed. A. Eide and M. Thee (New York: St. Martin's Press, 1980), 48.
18. C. J. Dunlap, "Melancholy Reunion: A Report from the Future on the Collapse of Civil-Military Relations in the United States," *USAF Institute for National Security Studies* (October 1996): 4.
19. Dunlap, "Melancholy Reunion," 11.
20. T. Marks, "Northern Ireland and Urban America on the Eve of the Twenty-first Century," in *Global Dimensions of High Intensity Crime and Low Intensity Conflict,* ed. G. Turbiville (Chicago: University of Illinois at Chicago, Office of International Criminal Justice, 1995), 77.
21. Marks, "Northern Ireland and Urban America," 79.
22. M. Feeley and J. Simon, "Actuarial Justice: The Emerging New Criminal Law," in *The Futures of Criminology,* ed. D. Nelken (Beverly Hills: Sage, 1994), 173–201; P. B. Kraska and V. E. Kappeler, "Militarizing American Police: The Rise and Normalization of Paramilitary Units," *Social Problems* 44 (1997): 1–18.
23. R. Bunker, "Street Gangs: Future Paramilitary Groups?" *Police Chief* (June 1996): 58.

The Military-Police Blur

———

3

The Thick Green Line

The Growing Involvement of Military Forces in Domestic Law Enforcement

___

Colonel Charles J. Dunlap Jr.

On 20 May 1997 a young American shot a Texas high school sophomore to death. Another instance of gang violence? No. In this case the shooter was a U.S. Marine on an antidrug patrol along the Rio Grande, a military operation that was part of a large border surveillance project conducted under the aegis of Joint Task Force 6 (JTF-6).[1] The marine mistook as a threat to his life, and that of the marines with him, the teenager who, though armed with a rifle, was merely tending a herd of goats. Although a subsequent investigation revealed that the shooting was a tragic culmination of mistakes and misperceptions, the incident served to awaken many Americans to the perils of employing the military for domestic security, a function historically the province of civilian law enforcement personnel.[2]

This essay briefly reviews the background of the use of the armed forces in a police capacity, discusses the growth of that role in the 1980s and 1990s, and forecasts an even greater expansion into that role in the near future due to the emerging threat of "catastrophic terrorism." I contend that this increased reliance on military resources for policing is not in the interest of either the armed forces or the public. Finally, I make some observations with a view toward minimizing the dangers of looking to the military to perform law enforcement tasks while ensuring the nation's public safety.

Background

Americans have traditionally viewed with suspicion the use of the armed forces for any sort of internal security purpose. These misgivings can be traced to an antipathy toward standing armies that is as old as the nation itself.[3] English colonists, cognizant of the excesses of Oliver Cromwell's New Model Army during the English Civil War, were wary of the nefarious potential of a professional military used at home. A further catalyst for this nascent antimilitarism arose when royal troops were employed to suppress the growing independence movement in the American colonies.[4]

Resistance to a law enforcement function for military forces hardly diminished following the American Revolution. Indeed, in framing the Constitution, one of the main aims was to limit the role of military forces in domestic activities. The final document provides relatively few authorities for employing the military within the nation's borders. Article 1, section 8, for example, allows Congress to provide for "calling forth the Militia to execute the Laws of the Union [and to] suppress Insurrections." Additionally, there is the language of article 4, section 4, which requires the federal government to protect the states against invasion and "on Application of the Legislature, or of the Executive (when the Legislature cannot be convened) against domestic Violence."

As is suggested above, the framers intended that the needs of national defense would be principally served by reliance not on full-time regulars but on part-time state-based militias. Even though the militia system seldom worked as originally designed, for much of the nation's history relatively small professional forces were augmented in wartime by huge increases in recruitment and conscription. Though this ad hoc approach met with mixed success in fighting the nation's wars, it essentially remained in place until the threat of the Soviet Union in the 1950s necessitated the maintenance of an enormous peacetime military establishment during the Cold War.

Consequently, there actually have been relatively few occasions where troops have functioned as "policemen" as that term is understood today. A major deviation from this norm took place during the Civil War era. Spurred by the Confederate insurgency, martial law was implemented in various areas of the North.[5] When this exercise of military power extended to the trial of civilians by military commission, the Supreme Court eventually intervened. In the case of *ex parte Milligan*, the court held that conducting such trials where the civil courts remained open was beyond the powers of the armed forces, despite the existence of a civil war.[6]

Nevertheless, federal troops were used extensively to police the South for over twenty years after the Civil War. Again, however, the wisdom of this strategy was questioned, this time by the legislative branch. According to one treatise, "Reconstruction era abuses, culminating in the use of federal troops to police polling stations in Southern States (some say to influence the outcome of the presidential election of 1876) led to the 1878 Posse Comitatus Act."[7] That act criminalizes any use of the armed forces to execute the laws except as may be specifically authorized by Congress.

Even though there has never been a prosecution for a violation of the Posse Comitatus Act, for the latter part of the nineteenth and all of the twentieth century, it served to limit the role of the military in anything resembling ordinary police work (except perhaps in the context of constabulary duties in frontier areas).[8] Of course, throughout U.S. history, military forces have been used to enforce civil law against domestic violence, mostly to suppress riots and similar civil disorders; in particular, troops were used on several occasions to counter labor unrest.[9] But such uses were exceptions to the general rule against the regular use of military force for police-like duties.

That paradigm began evolving in the early 1980s with the onset of the drug crisis. Cognizant of the international dimensions of the drug trade, convinced that local police forces were being overwhelmed by the problem, and impressed with the efficiency and renewed popularity of the armed forces, Congress passed a number of statutes designed to bring military resources to bear in the "war" on drugs. These statutes, still in effect today, permit the use of military equipment and expertise in support of civilian law enforcement agencies.[10] However, the law still prohibits a military member from "direct participation" in most circumstances in the "search, seizure, arrest, or other similar activity."[11] Separate legislative authority designates the Department of Defense (DOD) as the lead agency for the "detection and monitoring of aerial and maritime transit of illegal drugs into the United States."[12]

These strictures, however, do not necessarily limit the authority of state forces unless and until they are federalized. Included among such state forces is the National Guard, a hybrid organization having both state and federal status. This important legal distinction is often lost on a post–draft era public where fewer and fewer people have any firsthand knowledge of the military. Given that the guard's uniforms and equipment are virtually identical to that of the regular armed forces, this perception is wholly understandable. The ever more frequent use of guard personnel for drug operations and other law enforcement functions has the unintended consequence of serving to acclimate the public to the notion of uniformed military personnel performing such duties.

In any event, the end result of almost two decades of statutory change and billions of dollars in budgetary expenditures is the entrenchment of both regular and part-time military personnel in a variety of counterdrug efforts, including Joint Task Force 6.[13] In addition, there have been calls to use troops to augment police forces in high-crime, drug-infested urban areas.[14] More than anything else the drug problem has pushed the armed forces into institutionalized participation in law enforcement matters.

Counterdrug activities and the new statutes supporting them have also stimulated much collaboration between police and military forces. This has contributed to the "militarization" of police forces as they incorporate a wide range of military equipment into their inventories and turn to the military for advice and training.[15] In important ways we are witnessing a problematic convergence of police and military interests.

The Future

The involvement of the armed forces in what might be considered police or law enforcement activities is poised to increase exponentially in the near future. This is largely because of the growing threat of terrorism. While terrorism has a long history, consciousness of its dangers in the United States has risen markedly in the past few years. Bombings at New York's World Trade Center and Oklahoma City's Murrah Federal Building underlined terrorism's potential. Still, as destructive as those events were, they were efficiently investigated and the perpetrators quickly apprehended by law enforcement agencies with little help from the military.

But an even greater focus on terrorism was generated by the 1995 attack in Tokyo. In that event a religious cult released the deadly gas sarin in a subway, leaving twelve people dead and over twenty-five hundred injured. Such incidents have spawned fear of what is termed "catastrophic terrorism."[16] This insidious peril is usefully divided into two forms for purposes of this analysis: (1) that involving weapons of mass destruction (WMD), whether nuclear, biological, or chemical; and (2) that involving threats to microchip-based information and computer systems, so critical to modern societies.

With the new awareness has come new calls to use the armed forces to confront this unprecedented security challenge.[17] In a sense, the use of the military to confront these perils parallels the rationale for its use in the more traditional domestic role of suppression of civil disorders and even its newer role in drug interdiction. Specifically, the threats have the potential to overwhelm police resources, because of the emerging capability of a relatively small number of nonstate actors to use WMD to inflict casualties on a wartime scale.[18]

There have been a variety of DOD responses to the threat of catastrophic terrorism. Today, for example, the armed forces operate the Directorate of Military Support (DOMS) in the Pentagon. This organization serves as a nerve center for military involvement in all kinds of domestic activities ranging from the "Presidential inaugurations and Olympic Games to terrorist bombings and urban riots."[19]

In addition, the Pentagon is responsible for the Domestic Preparedness Program, an ambitious effort to train local police, fire, and medical personnel to deal with the dangers posed by biological and chemical devices.[20] Complementing this effort was the formation of several special military units to counter the WMD threat both at home and abroad.[21] In addition, the National Guard is organizing 170 reconnaissance and decontamination teams to respond to domestic WMD attacks.[22]

A related but somewhat different dilemma is presented by the threat to the nation's computer and communications systems. Many experts have long argued that the United States is extremely vulnerable to what has been called "cyberterrorism" or "information warfare."[23] In 1999 President Bill Clinton, following the recommendations of his Critical Infrastructure Protection Commission, sought $1.4 billion for his fiscal year 2000 budget to develop systems to protect the nation's banking, electric, transportation, and other critical industries.[24]

Cyberterrorism is an especially serious problem for the U.S. military, which is heavily dependent on computers for its daily operations and relies on many of the same microchip-based communication and electronic systems used by the general public.[25] Thus, wholly apart from any abstract desire to aid civilian law enforcement agencies, the armed forces have a very great interest in analyzing and defeating this kind of threat. That threat is

33

real: during an exercise in June 1997 it was discovered that DOD computer systems were far more vulnerable than had been previously thought.

As a consequence, the Pentagon recently announced the formation of a Joint Task Force Network Defense. This organization currently has the limited mission of defending DOD computers.[26] However, newly issued Pentagon doctrine suggests that protection of the nation's information infrastructure is properly a responsibility of DOD.[27]

The enormous scope of the threat of catastrophic terrorism has also generated suggestions for new organizations within the armed forces. A plan has been proposed—though scrapped for the moment—to establish a single military commander with authority to oversee domestic defense in the event of terrorist attack. According to press reports, this "homeland defense commander" would have "the know-how and authority to quickly dispatch technicians and troops, who could help deal with terrorist attacks that officials fear could inflict thousands of casualties and disrupt whole cities."[28]

The Emerging Issues

What we have seen in the last twenty years is a growing tendency to look to the armed forces to perform tasks that are essentially law enforcement. To many Americans the use of the military for these purposes is of little concern. The armed forces consistently lead public opinion polls as the most trusted institution in American society, topping even organized religion and the Supreme Court. Moreover, as John Hillen, then an analyst for the Heritage Foundation, put it in 1996: "Why do politicians want to use the military for police duties? To take advantage of one of the few parts of the federal government that actually works."[29]

Notwithstanding the seeming acquiescence of the public, this growing trend bears further analysis. In truth, there are few instances in modern times where the military effectively conducted a police-like internal security mission consistent with both the maintenance of an authentic combat capability and democratic values. That said, the issues with regard to using the armed forces for law enforcement can usefully be divided into practical problems and philosophical ones.

The Practical Problems
One of the principal reasons that many military leaders have long resisted employing their troops as police forces relates to the practical concern that

doing so diminishes combat prowess. Despite what the casual observer may think, there are surprisingly few synergies between law enforcement and military missions.

Examining the border shooting incident provides an illustration. There the Marine Corps insisted that the patrol acted in accordance with the "JTF-6 rules of engagement which include the inherent right of self-defense."[30] Though resolution of the specific facts of that case is beyond the scope of this article, it is easy to see how a dichotomy might arise. Military forces operating in a domestic situation, where the rules of engagement limit the use of force to "self-defense" situations, might still have an interpretation of the scope of the term that differs from that of local police forces. Under military practice, force may be used in self-defense to "decisively counter the hostile act or hostile intent and to ensure the continued safety of U.S. forces." Moreover, under certain conditions, engagement is permitted "until hostile force no longer presents an imminent threat."[31]

However, state law, not military doctrine, governs when military forces are acting domestically against civilian suspects outside of a federal enclave. Accordingly, the legal authority to use deadly force in such situations may be available to any citizen (as opposed to law enforcement officer) in a particular jurisdiction.[32] Thus, state legal requirements that mandate actions such as "retreat to the wall" before the use of deadly force is permitted are unknown in military practice and unlikely to be well understood by troops in the field.[33]

Indeed, using military forces for tasks that are essentially law enforcement requires a fundamental change in orientation. To put it bluntly, in its most basic iteration, military training is aimed at killing people and breaking things. Consequently, military doctrine has forces moving on a target by fire and maneuver with a view toward destroying that target. Police forces, on the other hand, take an entirely different approach. They have to exercise the studied restraint that a judicial process requires; they gather evidence and arrest "suspects." Where the military sees "enemies" of the United States, a police agency, properly oriented, sees "citizens" suspected of crimes but innocent until proven guilty in a court of law. These are two different views of the world.

Thus it is difficult for military personnel trained under a regime that emphasizes combat skills to align themselves with the more restrained procedure required for police work in a democratic society. When forced into such situations, military personnel tend to revert to the combat-oriented architecture that they understand and in which they are comfortable operating.

It is therefore not surprising that, for example, marine officers would characterize their deployment during the 1992 Los Angeles riots in the military language of "domestic peacekeeping." More troubling, but still comprehensible given their background and training, are reports that some marines "when faced with violating doctrine or violating federal law . . . chose the latter course."[34]

It is, of course, possible to train military personnel to suppress their previously instilled combat instincts to perform in the more restricted law enforcement environment. Once military personnel are converted into effective policemen, however, the very ethos that makes them succeed in combat has been dangerously eroded. The restraint so necessary for law enforcement could be catastrophic in war. Years before the 1997 JTF-6 incident, a colonel observing marines firing warning shots during a border skirmish with smugglers later argued that "combat-trained Marines shouldn't be diminishing hard-learned skills by squeezing off warning shots."[35]

Even when training succeeds in sufficiently purging military personnel of their combat skills, so that they conduct themselves appropriately as law enforcement agents, a significant and costly commitment must be made to retrain them back into war-fighting mind-set once those duties are completed. In an era of fewer and fewer troops and more and more commitments, commanders are understandably reluctant to do anything that saps combat readiness.

Another factor contributing to the reluctance of military commanders to become involved in law enforcement activities is the potential damage to morale and discipline that may result. It is mistaken to assume that individuals who join an all-volunteer force such as the U.S. military are necessarily inclined to perform domestic police duties. Quite obviously, if that were their personal preference they would have joined a police force. Moreover, while military personnel may be mentally well equipped to deal with a vicious battlefield adversary, they are rather less prepared to deal with a sophisticated criminal aiming to corrupt them.[36] Military leaders simply do not wish to expose their troops to this kind of harmful influence.

Additionally, military officers also believe that using military personnel for domestic law enforcement purposes carries great potential to harm civil-military relations. It can bring the military in conflict with civilian society and aggravate what many see as a growing estrangement of the military from the society it serves.[37] The uproar following the shooting in Texas is just one example. This may be one reason why the secretary of defense radically narrowed the circumstances under which such armed patrols might take place.[38]

But it is the emergence of "catastrophic terrorism" that portends the circumstance with the greatest potential to draw military personnel into domestic security situations. The immensity of threat necessitates military involvement, especially when WMD are involved, as only the armed forces have the infrastructure and training to meet the challenge of mass casualties. Moreover, other, technical aspects of catastrophic terrorism will likely pull military personnel into law enforcement duties more directly, although inadvertently.

Consider the menace of "cyberattack." It presents a particular conundrum for military officials because of the technical difficulty of distinguishing between assaults carried out by clever teenagers on a lark and those conducted by cyberterrorists and enemy nation-states bent on inflicting grievous damage to U.S. national security. Given that at the time of a particular assault on a DOD computer system, it may be impossible to know the identity of the attacker, military personnel could find themselves aggressively responding against a fellow citizen in a manner appropriate to a hostile foreign force but inconsistent with what an American rightly expects when merely suspected of a crime.

Conceiving of terrorists as criminals entitled to due process is not intuitive to military personnel or, for that matter, the terrorists themselves. Many terrorists and terrorist organizations like to portray themselves as "soldiers" engaged in "wars" against the United States and other mainly Western nations. However, both historical and current practice in the United States usually characterizes them as common criminals.[39] There are several reasons for this approach, not the least of which is the fact that under international law, lawful combatants in armed conflict are privileged from prosecution for violent acts that are otherwise in compliance with the law of war. In addition, combatants are entitled to POW status if captured.

Terrorists do not ordinarily achieve status as lawful combatants in armed conflict because the international law of war principally governs conflicts between nation-states and certain internationally recognized entities.[40] Though the law of war does apply to certain groups of irregular belligerents, terrorists also ordinarily fail to meet the minimum legal standards applicable to such forces, in that they fail to carry arms openly, wear a distinctive uniform or symbol, and subject themselves to internal military discipline aimed at enforcing the law of war.

In short, though they now may have the capability to inflict cataclysmic damage on the United States, the magnitude of their crimes does not per se transform terrorists into something other than criminals. Thus, perhaps the most formidable threat to U.S. interests in the future is, by its very nature, fundamentally a criminal challenge, albeit of unprecedented dimensions. This presents significant philosophical issues.

The Philosophical Issues

To be sure, philosophical reservations about the involvement of military personnel in law enforcement activities did not arise solely with the emergence of the challenge of catastrophic terrorism. Much concern has been expressed over the years about the military's drug control activities, and this uneasiness continues. Former secretary of the navy John Lehman wrote recently of the military's role in drug interdiction that "by accepting that new (and I believe unconstitutional) mission, the services have become de facto police. To involve the services in domestic law enforcement is to cross a dangerous line in separation of powers."[41]

In this connection it is worth remembering that the genius of the traditional American law enforcement system is that most police power is diffused among thousands of communities. Most of these more or less independent police agencies are subject to strict control by elected leaders at the local or state level. The civilian control of the military, however, is centralized in the president and national command authorities in Washington.[42] This system works well when confronting a foreign threat but markedly less well when employed domestically to interact with the citizenry, where force of arms is seldom the appropriate or necessary law enforcement tactic.

The troublesome potential of the enhanced role of the military in counterterrorism is generating the most criticism. Former secretary of defense Caspar Weinberger condemned the proposals by saying that they were "repugnant to democratic society."[43] Though there are no current plans to expand military authority into direct law enforcement (e.g., arrest/search authority), it is difficult to see how that could be avoided in a situation that would likely border on mass chaos.

The previously discussed proposal to appoint a single military commander for a "homeland defense" organization to handle such situations causes one critic to warn about the risk of "mission creep." Gregory T. Nojem, legislative counsel on national security for the American Civil Liberties Union, says, "The danger is in the inevitable expansion of that authority, so the military gets involved in things like arresting people and investigating crimes. . . . It's hard to believe that a soldier with a suspect in the sights is well positioned to protect that person's civil liberties."[44]

Concluding Observations

Obviously, those concerned with both civil liberties and domestic security are rightly apprehensive about the outcome of the current debates. One important step in setting the right course for the future would be establishing a clear definition of the kinds of threats manifesting a true national security threat, as opposed to those which present a law enforcement problem, recognizing, of course, that overlap can occur from time to time.

In considering this issue, it may be helpful to recall recent experience. As discussed above, during the 1980s and 1990s there was a major effort to transform the national drug issue into a national security threat suitable for the application of military force. Though military intrusion in what was essentially a law enforcement problem did grow, it fell short of full conversion of the armed forces to police work.

Today, we face another peril, that of catastrophic terrorism. This threat, if characterized as a national security risk, carries great potential to force that next step. No one should suffer the illusion that military forces could ever execute the laws with the same sensitivity to civil liberties as regular police forces. To do so is at odds with the central imperatives of military service. Moreover, a successful use of the armed forces for law enforcement may well render it incapable of defeating authentic external military threats.

What does the future hold? Secretary of Defense William Cohen warned in 1997 that "terrorism is escalating to the point that citizens of the United States may soon have to choose between civil liberties and more intrusive forms of protection."[45] That may be so, but employing military forces for internal security purposes will surely exacerbate the problem. Confronting terrorism requires, among other things, an intensive intelligence effort and aggressive investigative work. A military organization adept at destroying targets and undermining enemy command and control structures is not necessarily the best organization to do such work in a democracy.

It must be pointed out that in the American experience any call for using the armed forces for police work almost always arises from outside the military establishment. In the case of catastrophic terrorism, the lack of any immediate alternative complicates short-term solutions. In reporting the proposed terrorism-adapted "homeland defense" force, the *Washington Post* captured the essence of the dilemma:

> "Frankly, we are not seeking this job," said Deputy Secretary of Defense John Hamre. He acknowledged that "most Americans" are "apprehensive" about the military getting involved in domestic policing and crisis management. "But we know we're being asked to be involved because we have the only part of government that has the resources that can be mobilized," he added.[46]

A recent article in *Foreign Affairs* proposed a program for combating catastrophic terrorism that will require some of the intrusiveness about which Secretary Cohen warns and which Deputy Secretary Hamre recognizes.[47] Still, except for certain aspects of the draft National Terrorism Intelligence Center, it carefully excludes DOD from most activities in the law enforcement realm. (DOD would, however, have a large role in consequence management and preemptive and retaliatory strikes.) Similarly, a Justice Department proposal to take the lead from DOD in counterterrorism preparedness by 2001 appears to be the direction the evolution should take.[48] Although such proposals have real potential, considerable work is required for implementation. As these and other ideas are considered, it is vital that inertia and the penchant for quick fixes not allow responsibility for countering catastrophic terrorism to devolve permanently to the armed forces. The risks of doing so are great, and we should not be seduced by the absence in modern times of significant abuses by the armed forces. The stakes are very high. As Colonel Harry G. Summers, a decorated army veteran and expert on national security affairs, warns: "Like using fascism as a cure for the Great Depression, the involvement of military forces in civilian law enforcement could prove to be a greater assault on our democracy than any terrorist bombing, for it could destroy that democracy's very foundations."[49]

Notes

The views and opinions I present here are mine alone and do not necessarily represent those of the Department of Defense or any of its components. This chapter is a revised version of "The Police-ization of the Military," *Journal of Political and Military Sociology* 27, no. 2 (1999): 217–32.

1. Joint Task Force 6 is a multiservice organization whose mission is to provide surveillance for federal agents in border areas. "While not allowed to make arrests, they have carried out hundreds of observation sorties along the border, passing on information to the Border Patrol and drug-enforcement agents" (Sam Verhovek, "In Marine's Killing of Teenager, Town Mourns and Wonders Why," *New York Times,* 29 June 1997, 1, 12).
2. The marine responsible for the shooting was never prosecuted.
3. Laurie Keliman, "Domestic Anti-Terror Role for the Military Called Unnecessary," *Washington Times,* 11 May 1995, 6; Richard H. Kohn, *Eagle and Sword: The Federalists and the Creation of the Military Establishment in America, 1783–1802* (New York: Free Press, 1975), 3–9.
4. William S. Fields and David Hardy, "The Militia and the Constitution: A Legal History," *Military Law Review* 136 (1992): 9–13.
5. Charles Fairman, *Martial Law* (Chicago: Callaghan, 1943).
6. 71 U.S. 2 (1866); for a discussion of *Milligan* and other cases addressing civil liberties in wartime, see William H. Rehnquist, *All the Laws but One: Civil Liberties in Wartime* (New York: Knopf, 1998).
7. 18 U.S.C. §1385; Stephen Dycus, Arthur L. Berney, William C. Banks, and Peter Raven-Hansen, *National Security Law* (Boston: Little, Brown, 1990).
8. Following the siege at Wounded Knee, South Dakota, in 1973, plaintiffs seeking damages following a stand-off with a group of armed Indians argued that the army and the air force were used in violation of the Posse Comitatus Act. The court concluded that although military personnel did furnish advice and equipment, this did not constitute "execution" of the laws in violation of the act. In dicta, however, the court did observe that uses of the armed forces contrary to the act could result in a finding that evidence thereby obtained was inadmissible. *Rissonette v. Haig,* 776 F.2d 1384, affd, 800 F.2d 812 (8th Cir, 1986) (en bane), afd'd, 485 U.S. 264 (1988). Thus litigation involving the act occasionally appears but in the context of using it as an exclusionary rule, not as the basis for a criminal prosecution itself.
9. David E. Engdahl, "Soldiers, Riots, and Revolution: The Law and History of Military Troops in Civil Disorders," *Iowa Law Review* 1 (1971): 132–64.
10. See chapter 18 of title 10, U.S. Code.
11. 10 U.S.C. §375.
12. 10 U.S.C. §124.
13. Jim Garamone, "DoD Actively Supports Counterdrug Efforts," American Forces Information Service, November 1998, found at www.defenselink.mil/news/Nov1998/n11301998_9811303.html.
14. Catherine O'Neill, "Bring in the Army to End the Fear," *Los Angeles Times,* Washington ed., 29 March 1994, 1.
15. "Police Get Gadgetry Thanks to the Military," *Washington Post,* 30 November 1998, C4; Christopher M. Loder, "Cops Turn to West Point for Leadership Skills," *Newark Star-Ledger,* 28 April 1994, 35.
16. Flora Lewis, "The New Anti-Terrorism Is Scary," *International Herald Tribune,* 29 December 1998, 9.
17. For example, section 324(4) of Public Law 104-132 (cited at 22 U.S.C. §2377 note) states that Congress finds that "the President should use all necessary means, including covert action and *military force,* to disrupt, dismantle, and destroy international infrastructure used by international terrorists, including overseas training facilities and safe havens" (emphasis added).
18. Fred Bayles, "U.S. Police III: Prepared for Terror Attack," *USA Today,* 13 October 1998, 1.
19. Ernest Blazar, "Inside the Ring," *Washington Times,* 27 August 1998, 12.
20. See 10 U.S.C. §3 82. The effort reportedly has met with mixed success (Bayles, "U.S. Police III").
21. Bradley Graham, "U.S. Gearing Up against Germ War Threat," *Washington Post,* 14 December 1997, 1.

22. David Ruppe, "Guard to Play Major Counter-Terror Role," *Defense Week,* 19 October 1998, 1.
23. Winn Schwartau, *Information Warfare,* 2d ed. (New York: Thunder Mouth Press, 1996).
24. Heather Harreld, "Clinton: $1.4B to Fight Cyberterror," *Federal Computer Week,* 25 January 1999, 1.
25. Office of the Under Secretary of Defense for Acquisition and Technology, *Report of the Defense Science Board Task Force on Information Warfare-Defense* (November 1996).
26. Frank Wolfe, "Joint Task Force to Direct Pentagon's Cyber Defense," *Defense Daily,* 26 January 1999, 1.
27. Chairman of the Joint Chiefs of Staff, *Joint Doctrine for Information Operations,* Joint Publication 3-13 (9 October 1998).
28. Paul Richter, "Need for Anti-Terrorism Chief Debated," *Los Angeles Times,* 23 January 1999, 3.
29. John Hillen, "Don't Misuse the Armed Forces," *Investor's Business Daily,* 28 February 1996, 2.
30. Gary Martin, "Border Death Probe Branded Inadequate," *San Antonio Express-News,* 20 June 1998, 1.
31. Chairman of the Joint Chiefs of Staff, *Standing Rules of Engagement for U.S. Forces,* Instruction 3121.01, enclosure A, paragraphs 7 and 8 (1 October 1994).
32. Charles Torcia, ed., *Wharton's Criminal Law,* 14th ed. (Rochester, N.Y.: Lawyer's Co-Operative, 1979).
33. See Torcia, *Wharton's Criminal Law,* 126.
34. Thomas E. Ricks, "On American Soil: The Widening Gap between the U.S. Military and U.S. Society," in *Project on U.S. Post–Cold War Civil-Military Relations,* Working Paper no. 3, 21–22 (Cambridge, Mass.: John M. Olin Institute for Strategic Studies, Harvard University, May 1996).
35. Bill Torque and Douglas Waller, "Warriors without War," *Newsweek,* 19 March 1990, 18.
36. Indeed, some criminals have succeeded in corrupting military personnel; see, e.g., H. G. Reza, "A Drug Probe Finds Smugglers in the Military," *Los Angeles Times,* 13 December 1998, 1.
37. Ricks, "On American Soil," 21–22.
38. "Ground Troop Use on Border Curtailed, Officials Say," *Dallas Morning News,* 30 January 1999, 1.
39. At least one authority contends that some terrorists may also be considered unlawful combatants in an armed conflict; see Lt. Col. Richard J. Erickson, *Legitimate Use of Military Force against State-Sponsored International Terrorism* (Montgomery, Ala.: Air University Press, 1989).
40. This analysis is founded on both conventional (treaty) law and customary international law (*Air Force Pamphlet* 52A, 19 November 1976, 110–31).
41. John Lehman, "Our Military Condition," *American Spectator,* October 1998, 24.
42. Steven Wisotsky, "The War on Drugs and Civil Liberties," *USA Today Magazine,* July 1993, 17, 19.
43. Keliman, "Domestic Anti-Terror Role," 6.
44. William J. Broad and Judith Miller, "Pentagon Seeks Command for Emergencies in U.S.," *New York Times,* 28 January 1999, 1.
45. Patrick Pexton, "Banking on a Revolution," *Air Force Times,* 22 September 1997, 3; "Police Get Gadgetry."
46. Bradley Graham, "Pentagon Plans Domestic Terrorism Team," *Washington Post,* 1 February 1999, 2.
47. Ashton Carter, John Deutch, and Phillip Zelikow, "Catastrophic Terrorism: Tackling the New Danger," *Foreign Affairs,* November/December 1998, 80.
48. "Justice Department Poised to Take Pentagon's Counterterrorism Duties," *Inside the Pentagon,* 8 October 1998, 14.
49. Col. Harry G. Summers, "Using Military for Civilian Policing Bad Idea," *Stars and Stripes,* 10 May 1995, 17.

The Military Technostructures of Policing

Kevin D. Haggerty
Richard V. Ericson

The central and essential feature of the American Army of the 21st century will be its ability to exploit information.

General Gordon Sullivan, Chief of Staff, U.S. Army, 1995

Information is a critical feature of modern societies and it is the essential and central feature of policing.

Peter K. Manning, criminologist, 1992

The above quotations signal a convergence in the means by which the military and the police accomplish their different mandates. This convergence results in part from the movement into criminal law enforcement of electronic technologies for the production and distribution of knowledge useful in the administration of populations originally developed in military contexts.[1] These technologies have proven to be valuable not only for criminal law enforcement but also for surveillance in myriad other institutional contexts as they cohere with criminal law enforcement.[2] Such technology transfer constitutes an important and underexamined form of militarization of criminal justice. Where most discussions of militarization have concentrated on the influence of military discourse and models of organization, we suggest that these provide only a partial picture of militarization owing to their neglect of the most distinctive attribute of the contemporary military establishment, its scientific technostructure as part of the information age.

The predominant means through which military technologies have moved into wider society has been through a "trickle down" process. Recent political changes, however, have led to the emergence of a "directed" model of dispersion, characterized by active governmental attempts to spread military technoscientific products into other institutional realms. We examine these two models of technological militarization as they pertain to the public police and outline the affinity between such technologies and emergent actuarial policing practices.

While military institutions obviously vary considerably across nations, the focus here is on the United States. The United States exemplifies the changes in which we are interested. Moreover, as the dominant global military power, developments in America typically inform policies and practices in other countries. There are reasons to believe that irrespective of the size and scope of a nation's military, the technologies developed as part of the global military system, of which the United States is now the undisputed leader, will eventually permeate into far-flung criminal law enforcement. As such, our analysis is both an account of how criminal law enforcement has become militarized through surveillance technologies and a prediction about the future of policing.

Equipping the Military in the Information Age

The concept of "militarization" implies that another social institution assumes traits that are characteristic of the armed forces. In order to understand the process of militarization, therefore, one must first establish the distinguishing attributes of the armed forces and then proceed to detail how these characteristics influence other social institutions. We propose that the distinctive component of the contemporary military is its commitment to high technologies, and that militarization therefore involves the movement of such technologies into other institutional realms. From the development of the stirrup to the use of gunpowder, technological progress has been translated into battlefield advantage.[3] Since World War II, American military policy has been defined by a commitment to use advanced science and technology as the means to secure military superiority.[4] Not content to be the beneficiary of sporadic scientific progress, the armed forces have directed science to address specific military concerns. As a result, much of the U.S. scientific establishment has become a de facto extension of the military complex. In his survey of transformations to scientific institutions, Dickson goes so far as to conclude that the remarkable scientific growth experienced during the Cold War was "as much the result of a largely accidental spin-off from the arms race as a reflection of a conscious political desire to promote science for its own (or society's) sake."[5]

The institutional contours of this military/technoscience union were formalized in the 1950s and 1960s, when new military laboratories and think tanks were established and military funds were poured into specialized projects and basic research. Among the major beneficiaries of these developments were the universities, private corporations, individual scientists, and some specific scientific disciplines in which the military invested heavily.[6] In the two decades after World War II the Office of Naval Research funded approximately half of the U.S. students taking doctorates in the physical sciences.[7] In 1954 the Department of Defense and Atomic Energy Commission combined to account for 96 percent of all university physics research supported by federal funds.[8] Similar patterns continue to the present day. In 1994, $30 billion, or roughly 70 percent of total federal research and development expenditures, were dedicated to military initiatives.[9]

The range of tools that have been developed through military research efforts extends well beyond lethal devices. In particular, military research is responsible for the highly sophisticated communication and surveillance systems that now make up the military's backbone. As such, the designation "military technology" can be properly applied to the expanded network of nonlethal artifacts that the military has helped to create. Moreover, it was inevitable that such an extensive and directed scientific effort would pervade institutions beyond the military.

In the "trickle down" view, technologies produced to meet military needs spread into wider society largely as a result of the efforts of the corporations that, with military support, have developed them. In this view, the state does little to ensure that these tools are adopted in other contexts. In fact, the state may even seek to encumber the distribution of some forms of knowledge and technology in order to maintain at least a temporary military advantage. In contrast, in the "directed" model, the state makes explicit attempts to ensure that such technologies move into different institutional settings. Figure 4.1 schematically displays these two different models as they apply to policing. These two models can be used to describe the state's approach to the dispersion of any particular artifact, including military tech-

Figure 4.1
Two Models of Military Technoscientific Dispersion

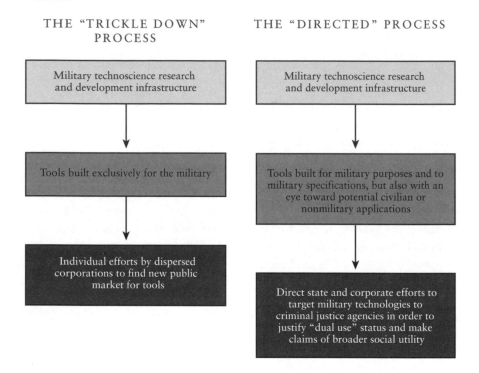

THE "TRICKLE DOWN" PROCESS

THE "DIRECTED" PROCESS

Military technoscience research and development infrastructure

Military technoscience research and development infrastructure

Tools built exclusively for the military

Tools built for military purposes and to military specifications, but also with an eye toward potential civilian or nonmilitary applications

Individual efforts by dispersed corporations to find new public market for tools

Direct state and corporate efforts to target military technologies to criminal justice agencies in order to justify "dual use" status and make claims of broader social utility

nologies. As we demonstrate in the final section, the American government has now clearly adopted a "directed" policy that seeks to transfer a wide range of military technology into criminal justice.

The history of the computer is a succinct and perhaps paradigmatic example of the "trickle down" movement of a military technology into wider society. While it may at first seem odd to designate the computer a military technology, its genesis is deeply entwined in military interests. Before World War II the little research that was being conducted on computing machines lacked a unifying mandate and frequently took place in basement and kitchen laboratories. With the outbreak of war, the military supplied the urgency, specifications, market, and massive amounts of funds required to galvanize the development of the computer. Some of the first uses for these early prototypes included the calculation of ballistic trajectories, the design of lenses for aircraft reconnaissance photography, and calculations on implosion as part of the research on the production of the atomic bomb. After

World War II, responsibility for computer development was turned over to the private sector, but it continued to be shaped by military interests, imperatives, and funds.[10] A few quantitative indicators provide an impression of the extent of the armed forces' influence on the field of computing during this period. In the 1960s the military consumed 70 percent of the microchips produced, and in 1985 the U.S. Department of Defense spent $14 billion on computers, a figure that had doubled by 1990.[11] By 1989 there was over a third of a million computers in the Pentagon's inventory.[12]

Hand in hand with this computerization has emerged a new military ideology that emphasizes the strategic importance of information. While information has long been recognized as delivering wartime advantages, the contemporary armed forces are distinctive by virtue of their prioritization of information above all else. This new vision of warfare is enshrined in the Pentagon's new philosophies of "mid-intensity" and "low-intensity" conflict.[13] While conflicts may have become "low intensity," they are decidedly high technology. Such policies involve a commitment to maintaining technological superiority over regional powers through the integration of complex communications infrastructures, visualization tools, and unimaginable amounts of data.[14] The "coming out" party for this vision of technowarfare was the Gulf War, which, with the almost giddy support of the media, was constructed "as an advertisement for continuation of U.S. dominance in military high technology."[15]

Despite the heady proclamations of military superiority that flowed in the wake of the Gulf War, this style of conflict has also raised some troubling concerns. First, it has become apparent that rather than having rendered the store of military information more manageable, computers have resulted in the production of ever more information, provoking demands for still more computers, "in an escalating spiral to which there [is] no clear logical end."[16] The sheer volume of information, and the speed at which it must now be processed, has also prompted efforts to divest humans of decision-making responsibility and invest it onto computers themselves. In pursuit of that goal the military has heavily supported research on artificial intelligence. Such an increased reliance on computers has in turn raised questions about the vulnerability of the information system itself.[17] In a May 1998 lecture, President Bill Clinton warned about the new threats posed to the United States and proposed that "rather than invading our beaches or launching bombers, these adversaries may attempt cyber-attacks against our critical military systems and our economic base."[18]

The computer, then, is a prime example of a technology whose genesis and development have been shaped by military interests. To varying degrees we could trace a comparable influence on a range of other technologies, including lasers, nuclear energy, encryption devices, satellites, the Internet, biometrics, virtual reality, sensors, optics, radar, and an incalculable number of largely invisible component parts and forms of expertise that make these tools function. With few governmental initiatives specifically designed to promote such technology transfer, these tools have entered many areas of institutional life. In the process, they have helped transform existing practices and ideologies.

"Trickle Down" Effects on Policing

The philosopher Michel Foucault has suggested that the eighteenth century was shaped by a military dream of the perfect society.[19] The military training of that time involved breaking down the actions of individual soldiers into a series of discrete smaller steps. These were then practiced repeatedly under the scrutiny of superiors until they became second nature, as exemplified by the practice of military drill. Consequently, the military dream of the perfect society consisted of the "meticulously subordinated cogs of a machine," "permanent coercions," "indefinitely progressive forms of training," and "automatic docility." Contemporary transformations in military technoscience have helped to supplant this vision of the military. The twenty-first century promises to be shaped by a new militaristic dream that involves a quest for immediate, perfect, and total knowledge and absolute command at a distance, all combined with the ability to transcend human limitations on perception.

In this section we relate how police practice and ideology are changing, partially as a result of its embrace of military-inspired high technology. To the extent that many of these technologies have their origins in military research and development, they have moved into policing largely on the "trickle down" model of dispersion. Their appeal to the police derives from the way in which they reinforce and augment managerial and governmental practices. As such, they are the technological conditions of possibility for the expansion and intensification of a model of policing that accentuates the routine surveillance of populations, scrutiny of data banks, and communication of risk knowledge to a host of agencies external to the police.[20]

This style of policing is dramatically at odds with popular conceptions of how police officers spend their time. The public face of the police accentuates an image of officers involved in the investigation of crimes and the pursuit, capture, and processing of criminals. While such imagery provides the police with their public legitimacy, it also dramatically misrepresents the bulk of their work. Contrary to televised representations, police officers are seldom involved in such conventional endeavors. In Canada, for example, a police officer records on average one indictable crime occurrence a week, makes one indictable crime arrest every three weeks, and secures one indictable crime conviction every nine months.[21] Even in New York City, which at the time of research by Walsh had an extraordinarily high rate of serious crime, officers were found to spend an extraordinarily small amount of time dealing with crime and capturing criminals.[22] Among 156 patrol officers assigned to a high-crime area, Walsh found that 40 percent did not make a single felony arrest in a year and 69 percent made no more than three felony arrests in a year.

If stereotypical "crime busting" work does not comprise an officer's routine workload, in what type of enterprise are police officers engaged? Research on the public police has demonstrated that the vast majority of an officer's time is consumed by different forms of surveillance or knowledge work.[23] Much of this work involves efforts to document the disparate events and situations the police are called upon to deal with, and the scope of this enterprise can be overwhelming. The Royal Canadian Mounted Police, for example, have over two thousand operational forms, some of which contain hundreds of possible classificatory options. A single incident can necessitate the production of more than a dozen forms, each containing substantially different information demanded by a range of institutional audiences, such as private insurance, customs, the courts, statistical agencies, health organizations, regulatory organizations, and educational and financial institutions. As such, the police are a central hub in an extended network of knowledge production and dissemination.

The organizations that have negotiated access to this police-generated information employ it as the cornerstone of governmental strategies to manage the aggregate populations for whom they are responsible. Such strategies are increasingly a routine component of criminal justice, signaling a change toward a system of "actuarial justice," which is characterized by the use of techniques to manage aggregate populations through risk assessment techniques.[24] The police role increasingly involves documenting behavior and events, and disseminating this knowledge as required by assorted risk institutions. Their practices in this regard include the visual observation of people and places as well as the routine production and scrutiny of bureaucratic data.

It is in this context of actuarial justice that we must understand the appeal of high technology to the police. While by no means as technology-laden as the military, police organizations have at their disposal a considerable infrastructure of science and technology that includes dispatch systems, forensics, computerized reporting systems, databases, and a large assortment of other surveillance tools.[25] Such technologies hold out the promise of efficiency gains in both the management of populations and the management of police knowledge systems themselves.

To flesh out some of the linkages between this model of policing and military high technology, we can return to the example of the computer, the military genesis of which we have already mentioned. Computers have been used in policing for decades to manage administrative tasks, but they are increasingly a component of law enforcement's operational arm. And while the following examples are not representative of the technological capabilities of all police forces, they provide an appreciation for the possibilities computers provide the police and certainly signal the direction in which many police forces are likely to move.

Law enforcement agencies have computerized many of their former paper-and-pencil criminal records systems. In the process they have acquired significant gains in the speed of information retrieval and size of data holdings. Again, some quantitative indicators provide an appreciation for the scope of such databases. The British Police National Computer contains 50 million records on vehicle owners and stolen and suspect vehicles. Eleven million people are checked against this database every year.[26] In 1989 the U.S. federal National Crime Information Center (NCIC) contained more than 20 million records and handled 1 million transactions a day.[27] New computers have meant speedier checks. And while enhancements in computer speed can be difficult to measure, Burnham reports on a study that documents how in 1980 FBI computers could achieve approximately 5.3 million instructions per second.[28] Ten years later they were more than forty times faster, a surge in computer power that was almost twice that achieved by the Social Security Administration and ten times that of the Internal Revenue Service during the same period.

The ease of reporting that computers allow has also contributed to an expansion in the amount of information that police officers collect, as categories of information that might previously have been ignored are now saved on a "just in case" basis. For example, our research documents how one unanticipated consequence of the introduction of in-car reporting systems is the tendency of officers to record additional information on victims and witnesses.[29] In Europe, such computer-enhanced expansion of information collection has been institutionalized at the transnational level, where the European Police Office is now permitted to collect data on suspected criminals, victims, witnesses, and anyone else who might be able to provide relevant information. This mandate gives them a "de facto authority to collect data on anybody."[30] And the range of information they record can itself be disturbing. In the United Kingdom, for example, police records can include racial origin, political opinion, health, sexual life, and criminal convictions.[31]

Increased availability of computers has also contributed to the development of "database policing," where patrol officers routinely search computers to scrutinize various attributes pertaining to a person, vehicle, residence, or business in the hopes of getting a "hit." This practice can be even more pronounced among detectives who spend still more of their time checking various databases.[32] Furthermore, through computer matching techniques, the authorities can be automatically notified every time an individual is engaged in certain combinations of electronically recorded behaviors.[33] The police mania for information appears to reach its height in Central Scotland, where a regional police force has adopted a comprehensive police computer system:

> Phone conversations, reports, tip-offs, hunches, consumer and social security databases, crime data, phone bugging, audio, video and pictures, and data communications are inputted into a seamless GIS [geographic information system], allowing a relational simulation of the time-space choreography of the area to be used in investigation and monitoring by the whole force. The Chief Constable states: "What do we class as intelligence in my new system in the force? Everything! The whole vast range of information that comes into the possession of a police force during a twenty-four hour period will go on to my corporate database. Everything that every person and vehicle is associated with.[34]

But even this extreme example does not capture the extent to which police work has been computerized. With the general societal proliferation of computers, the police now have more resources at their disposal to monitor and retrospectively reconstruct individual behavior. Police organizations have secured routine, and often informal, access to a host of nonpolice databases, such as those from insurance companies and financial institutions. Research by Northrop, Kramer, and King indicates that the police have become the primary users of many systems originally established for other governmental purposes, and Gordon reports on proposals to link the federal NCIC police database to computers from Social Security, Internal Revenue, Passport, Securities and Exchange, and the State Department.[35] In some Southern California communities the police now have direct computerized access to school records.[36]

In surveying the informational horizon in search of ever more potentially useful sources, police organizations have recently recognized the surveillance and investigative potentials provided by enormous corporate databases. Files from telephone and utilities companies can be used to document an individual's lifestyle and physical location, and marketing firms have developed consumer profiling techniques that contain precise information on a person's age, gender, political inclinations, religious preferences, reading habits, ethnicity, family size, income, and so on.[37] When these sources are combined through practices of computerized data matching, they allow for exponential increases in the amount of information the police have at their disposal. The FBI has already employed commercial databases for undisclosed investigative purposes, and the federal Drug Enforcement Agency has developed its own in-house registry with information culled from mailing and telephone listings, direct marketers, voter records, and assorted commercial sources.[38] Although cloaked in secrecy, this registry was expected to contain 135 million records as of its inception in 1991 and would subsequently receive regular updates of corporate and residential data. Cumulatively, the societal proliferation of databases is rapidly transforming the police system into a host of policing systems—interconnected computer networks that are differentially available to public and private law enforcement officials.

This policing information explosion has been accompanied by some of the same problems of data overload and system complexity that now plague the military. The FBI in particular faces being overwhelmed by wiretap and transactional data. In an attempt to resolve this problem the bureau has turned to another set of technologies that has been shaped by military interests, artificial intelligence and expert systems. The FBI now employs a multidomain expert system (MDS) to analyze the reams of data that course through their agency, and research is ongoing into the prospect of employing artificial intelligence to reproduce the investigative strategies of police detectives.[39] In an attempt at systems integration reminiscent of an air force fighter cockpit, the Texas Transportation Institute has won awards from Vice President Al Gore and a major computer magazine for its prototype of the police car of the future. This vehicle includes a computerized touch screen that integrates assorted police technologies. From this single interface officers can access radar, magnetic strip and bar code readers, license plate readers, an enhanced video camera/recorder, and a global positioning system/vehicle locator. This special police car also comes equipped with a mobile hand-held unit that allows officers to remotely contact the police communications center, complete and submit reports, send and receive text and graphic data, and query various federal, state, and local databases.[40]

These instances of police computerization are cumulatively but one example, albeit an important one, of the "trickle down" movement of military technology into policing. Other militarily influenced technologies, both large and small, have contributed to the development of an actuarial, risk-management style of policing. For example, we are now familiar with the use of surveillance cameras in corner stores, malls, and sports and entertainment complexes. Increasingly, these cameras are moving into the public streets, as more cities subject their downtown core to constant surveillance. While several U.S. cities have embraced such efforts, the United Kingdom has been the leader among Western nations in their attempts to surveil the city.[41] It has reached the point that a city dweller in Britain can now expect to be caught on film every five minutes.[42] The British government has recently granted a research team at the University of Bristol's experimental psychology department fifty thousand pounds to develop a system to predict in real time when a crime is about to occur. This will be accomplished by scrutinizing existing CCTV tapes and determining which recorded behaviors and gestures tend to precede crimes. This knowledge will then be embedded in a computer program that will alert the police when CCTV cameras record such behavior on the street, prompting police targeting and intervention before a crime has actually taken place.[43] Such efforts have a clear military lineage. For example, the British leadership in the area of CCTV can be traced in part to the several decades of experimentation with electronic counterinsurgency and antiterrorist city planning conducted in Belfast by the British army and in efforts to secure London from IRA threats.[44]

Thanks to military technoscience, law enforcement agencies can now also look to the sky to augment their surveillance capabilities. Satellites and geographic positioning systems with direct military roots now subject the earth to a mind-boggling level of scrutiny. While the exact specifications of such satellites are classified, we can extrapolate from the capabilities demonstrated during the Gulf War to suggest that the military's minimum satellite photographic capability is six inches in diameter, and very likely much smaller.[45] In 1997 the first civilian spy satellite was launched that uses declassified spy technology to allow customers to request pictures over the Internet. These can display features as small as three meters across.[46] Law enforcement agencies already use satellite reconnaissance to police rural areas and detect drug crops. The United Nations recently agreed to establish high-technology monitoring of the earth that will include ground surveys and remote satellite sensing in an attempt to eradicate drug planting by the year 2008. The agricultural uses of such images have extended to the identification of lawns that were being watered too much during the 1990 drought in Southern California.[47] More conventional criminal investigations can also employ such images, evidenced by the fact that the Los Angeles Police Department approached a commercial company to obtain satellite photographs in an effort to determine whether O. J. Simpson's infamous white Bronco was outside Nicole Brown's home on the night of the murders.[48]

"Directed" Effects on Policing

Richard Quinney coined the phrase the "criminal justice industrial complex."[49] In so doing, he self-consciously echoed Dwight Eisenhower's celebrated caution that "we must guard against the acquisition of unwarranted influence, whether sought or unsought, by the military industrial complex." Quinney's concern, however, was less with the military than with what he saw as the alliance being forged between the criminal justice establishment and corporations that require markets for technologies of social control. Recent political transformations should prompt us to reflect further on the original military inspiration for Quinney's caution, as there is now evidence that criminal justice is being targeted as never before as a market for military high technology.

In the previous section we documented how the military has influenced police work, especially through the case of computerization, in a "trickle down" process of technological dispersion. In recent years, however, there has been a change toward a more "directed" approach to technology transfer. The reasons behind this development are related to broader political transformations, the most important being the disintegration of the Cold

War threat after the collapse of the Soviet Union in 1989. These political transformations produced myriad rippling effects, some of which are now being felt in police work. One almost immediate effect was that the funding for the U.S. military's technoscience infrastructure, which previously had the political status of a sacred cow, was increasingly portrayed as a fattened cow rightfully headed for slaughter. Although there have been few determined attempts to beat swords into plowshares, discussion has taken place about the possibility of a peace dividend, as politicians contemplate ways in which to direct military funds toward domestic concerns.

Such developments have not been welcome news to the state legislatures and powerful military technoscience institutions, which have jointly come to depend on free-flowing federal defense dollars. What emerged from the wrangling on Capitol Hill over funding for military research and development was a compromise position, one that would direct some of the military technological benefits into wider society but maintain military priorities and agendas over the development of these technologies. These have included efforts to direct the research and development conducted in existing agencies toward more civilian concerns, or more commonly, toward "dual use" technologies. President Clinton made it a cornerstone of his administration to fund the development of such dual-use technologies, which are designed to have both military and civilian applications.[50] While they are ostensibly joint military/civilian ventures, such initiatives remain largely under Pentagon control because of the stipulation that they have military relevance.[51]

Given the perceived affinity between the military and criminal law enforcement, it is perhaps not surprising that the police have been singled out as one of the beneficiaries of the development of such dual-use technologies. A complex array of programs and institutions has rapidly been established to further this goal. In 1994 the U.S. Department of Justice and the Department of Defense entered into a Memorandum of Understanding on "Operations Other Than War," which sought to develop technologies valuable to both agencies. This initiative led to the creation of five law enforcement technology centers designed to apply advanced war-fighting technology to criminal justice.[52] The Department of Defense also operates the Advanced Research Projects Agency (ARPA), which oversees the Technology Reinvestment Program and the Advanced Technology Program, both of which are involved in attempts to develop dual-use technologies. A "government technology transfer program" has been established to enable the Department of Defense and commercial organizations to assist law enforcement through the application of defense-related technology. In 1996 the National Institute of Justice entered into partnership agreements with the Departments of Defense and Energy and the Border Research and Technology Center to share technology and resources.

Federal funds have been secured to direct military technology into criminal justice. Congress appropriated $37.5 million of the defense budget in 1995, and $30 million in 1996, to support the conversion of military technology to law enforcement uses. In addition, the "Schroeder Amendment" to the 1994 Crime Act dedicated 1 percent of policing money to the development of technology: this amounts to approximately $20 million dedicated to research on police technology over three years. The author of this amendment, U.S. Representative Patricia Schroeder, has been a strong proponent of using military technology in law enforcement. Schroeder also demonstrates how the rhetoric of "suitable enemies" can still be mobilized toward the enhancement of technological resources: "During the Cold War we were worried about enemies that were far away. But now there are enemies among us. The whole security thrust is changing."[53]

A 1996 conference sponsored by the National Law Enforcement and Corrections Technology Center provides further evidence of the new military, political, and technological character of law enforcement. Sponsored by the American Defense Preparedness Association, an educational association that arranges partnerships between the military and industry for the purpose of developing defense products, the conference addressed the potential uses of technology, particularly military technology, in criminal justice. Some of the items discussed included assorted surveillance tools, such as remotely piloted vehicles, X rays, video cameras, and myriad sensors. There was also talk about the use of tracking and personal-identification systems, computer databases, and electronic networks and the prospects of employing virtual reality to train officers. One of the keynote speakers, Colonel J. Boone, USAF Vice Commander, Space and Missile Systems Center, catalogued some of the military technologies that his agency has tested for law enforcement purposes, including a laser illuminator, an infrared-sensitive camera, and a telephoto lens mounted with a night vision scope. Congresswoman Jane Harrnan also addressed the meeting and recounted how as a traditional center for the aerospace industry, her California congressional district had recently fallen on difficult financial times. Consequently, she believed that the transfer of defense technology to law enforcement would benefit all parties involved, and that "more money to purchase critical technology means less wasted police time, more and quicker apprehensions and more public safety." Perhaps most importantly for a politician, she continued, "this also means a new and important market for our local industrial base."[54]

Some military/law enforcement organizational hybrids have already produced results. Consider the Rapid Prototyping Facility in Quantico, Virginia. Jointly operated by the FBI and ARPA, in 1994 it received $5.4 million to employ computer-aided design, engineering, and manufacturing tools to develop miniature microphones, cameras, and concealment packages. One of its more impressive products is a mobile automobile tracking system that can be set up in any metropolitan area. It employs a grid of hidden sensors scattered through the city to allow for a second-by-second tracking of electronically tagged vehicles. Although designed to be portable, the system has been established on a permanent basis in New York City.[55]

The FBI has worked closely with the Department of Defense's National Security Agency to lobby for legislation to enhance official wiretapping capabilities. They have also joined forces in efforts to discourage the use of commercially available encryption technologies and to advocate for the use of encryption devices that still allow the government to monitor ostensibly private telephone and Internet communications.[56] The policing of the Internet now offers greater opportunities for the technological melding of policing and the military. For example, the U.S. Defense Department recently opened a $15 million high-tech computer lab dedicated to controlling computer crime. Authorities anticipated that this resource would be shared with domestic policing authorities and allowed the FBI to establish its own mini-lab upstairs in the facility.[57] In addition, the federal government's inelegantly named "1033 Program" promises to transfer a considerable amount and variety of military hardware directly into police work. Established in 1989, this program provides law enforcement agencies with excess military hardware free of charge. By 1996 police forces had already obtained equipment worth $336 million in this manner. The range of technologies that have been made available include clothes, radios, gas masks, tractor-trailers, sniper rifles, aircraft, helicopters, and armored personnel carriers.[58]

The specifics of how these new military and law enforcement amalgamations will evolve remain unclear. However, any residual skepticism about the links between law enforcement and military technoscience should be removed by contemplating the following list. Drawn from the National Institute of Justice's website, it consists of a partial summary of military-affiliated technologies that are currently being developed or evaluated for potential law enforcement applications by the NIJ's National Law Enforcement and Corrections Technology Center. The list includes a diagnostic system for explosive devices jointly sponsored by the Departments of Justice and Defense; a device to detect the heartbeat of individuals hiding in vehicles that was initially part of the nuclear weapons counterproliferation program; an in-car voice verification system targeted for use at the U.S.-Mexico border and created by a research team that includes the Air Force Research Laboratory; a device to identify airborne chemicals used in the manufacture of methamphetamine that employs technology derived from the military's chemical warfare detector; a device produced by Raytheon (formerly Hughes Missile Systems) that employs radar to see and track individuals through brick walls; a series of ground sensors designed to detect human intrusion that are being funded by the Office of Naval Research's Domestic Technology Transfer Program; and an evaluative study by the Air Force Research Laboratory of commercial voice stress analysis technology for military and law enforcement purposes.

This already impressive list continues with a study of the applicability of the "Dragonfly" Information Security Product. Originally developed for the Department of Defense, the "Dragonfly" consists of a network of security products that ensure data confidentiality, access control, authentification, and data integrity. A Speech Enhancement Unit to reduce noise interference on radios and telephones is being developed in conjunction with the Air Force Research Laboratory. A Time Line Analysis System is being tested for use as a police investigative tool, following its original use by the Department of Defense to provide analytic and visualization tools in support of foreign command and control systems. A Computer Forensics Kit based on defensive information warfare technology is being studied for potential uses in preserving information to ensure computerized audit trails for police investigation and prosecution. An evaluation of "tele-forensics" is being conducted by a research team that includes the Army Medical Research and Material Command to explore the possibility of providing forensic experts with remote access to crime scenes through the integration of video teleconferencing and communications technology. And last, but by no means least, a joint NASA and National Institute of Justice project is studying the prospect of creating technologies that will be beneficial to both agencies. Included in this project are portable imaging and remote sensing tools, neutron/gamma-ray spectroscopy, and advanced data networks. NASA anticipates that some of these technologies will be field-tested during crime scene investigations.

While it is commonly assumed that technologies are designed to solve specific problems, the above list suggests that the converse can also be true;

that new problems can be sought for existing technologies. This appears to be what is happening in criminal justice, as military technoscience, now facing pressures to justify products in terms of a broader social utility, has turned to criminal justice as an easy source of legitimacy. The broad social remit of criminal justice, combined with an actuarial ideology that predisposes the police to embrace such technologies, makes criminal justice an attractive site in which to advocate on behalf of the "dual use" capabilities of military technologies. Indeed, there seems to be few surveillance, communications, or computation systems that, given sufficient ingenuity, could not be enlisted in some facet of the "war" against crime.

Conclusions

The military influence on police work does not necessarily arrive donned in helmet and jackboots, but can appear clad in the more reassuring attire of lab coat or business suit. In this concluding section we take the opportunity to introduce some clarifying points about how this form of militarization should be understood. We also briefly address the possibility that financial constraints might stand in the way of the police's adopting such technologies.

First, our focus on technology should not be taken as a technologically determinist futurology that heralds the immanent arrival of RoboCop forms of policing. The adoption of these technologies is bound to be accompanied by problems of system incompatibility, officer resistance, and data glut. It is entirely likely, however, that solutions to these problems will be sought through the introduction of yet more technology. And rather than these accumulated technologies radically transforming the mandate of the police at the outset, they are apt to be used to further traditional policing practices to whatever extent possible. We have stressed that much police work involves efforts to document myriad events for various institutional audiences and conduct routine forms of bureaucratic and optical surveillance of different populations (including police officers themselves). It is in their ability to intensify and rationalize such processes that these new technologies are apt to be most attractive to police officials.[59]

Furthermore, our focus on communication technology and surveillance is not meant to dismiss other components of police practice. In particular, we do not suggest that communication technologies have superseded coercive technologies by making them, in effect, redundant. Instead, communication technologies allow for the rationalization of the use of force by further entrenching a continuum of violence, one that involves subtle gradations in official response that range from routine bureaucratic documentation of behavior to more coercive interventions. Between these two extremes are a host of more directed forms of surveillance and a subtle escalation in technologically assisted violence, most readily apparent in the police embrace of new "less than lethal" technologies.

The introduction of such communication technologies into policing is not the harbinger of a totally controlled society. What we appear to be witnessing is the emergence of a society where both surveillance and the public awareness of such surveillance are increasingly the norm. This reflexive public appreciation of surveillance can introduce a dynamic interplay between the watchers and the watched. Even as the optics of these new technologies become more refined, people search out spaces (both physical and informational) beyond official scrutiny and attempt to creatively turn the gaze back upon the official watchers.[60]

Given the attractions of such technologies to the police, it would appear that the single greatest impediment to their adoption is financial. Indeed, many of these systems are expensive, often prohibitively so. However, we want to suggest briefly several reasons why we anticipate that despite these costs, funds will probably be found to further such technology transfer.

First, although the past two decades have been characterized by a general pattern of fiscal retrenchment in state governments, criminal law enforcement has been largely exempt from such cutbacks.[61] Speaking in 1995, Deputy Attorney General Jamie Gorelic boasted that since 1988 the investment in law enforcement and criminal justice has grown at roughly twice the rate of all other government spending. As a sign of the times, she then proceeded to urge her audience that in order to confront crime they must "use Defense Department technology as a force multiplier."[62]

Second, rather than being portrayed as an expense, new technologies are frequently rationalized as being able to produce long-term cost savings. Cameras, computers, and sensors ostensibly free up officers to do more work or allow more routine police tasks to be entirely automated.

Third, as computerized police tools continue to standardize and routinize many police functions, they also offer the prospect of achieving further savings by transferring more police tasks to the private sector, an undisputed growth area in policing.[63] While new forms of "database policing" require expensive efforts to establish and maintain these systems, police organizations are responsible for only a fraction of the databases that officers might have cause to search. The rest are managed by corporate institutions or other governmental agencies, with the police being an unanticipated beneficiary of these expanded stores of information.

Fourth, we should emphasize that powerful military and corporate interests lie behind these new technologies. Such industries have demonstrated an unparalleled ability to secure governmental funds. Given the federal government's new funding structures, many of their lobbying efforts will undoubtedly be directed toward policing to justify the dual-use status of their technologies. Over the past several decades, the military-industrial complex has done much to disabuse us of the notion that there might be rational limits to the amount of public money that can be spent on military science and technology.

While we have accentuated the direct and indirect influence of military technoscience on police work, it should be borne in mind that other institutions are also being shaped by this form of militarization. Indeed, it has become a conscious legitimization strategy of the extended military technoscience complex to advocate in terms of the wider social benefits that accrue from military research and development. And there is truth to such claims, as many of the technologies we now embrace for their ability to shrink the globe, improve health, and provide entertainment might not have developed at all, or at least not in the same way, if not for the direction and urgency that military interests have been able to bring to science.

It can be disconcerting to acknowledge the extent to which technologies we now take for granted have their roots in enterprises that are often unpalatable. Virilio and Lotringer succinctly highlight this normative ambiguity when they observe that "war is generally considered a negative phenomenon, and technology a positive one. So to say that the positive phenomenon of technology came in large part from the arsenal and war economy is already hard for people to accept."[64] In light of the current efforts to direct military technologies into domestic realms, we are left with the prospect of still greater normative confusion as the technologies designed to make war possible weave their way into the social fabric that makes society possible.

Notes

This chapter is a revised version of "The Militarization of Policing in the Information Age," *Journal of Political and Military Sociology* 27, no. 2 (1999): 233–56.

1. Christopher Dandeker, *Surveillance, Power, and Modernity: Bureaucracy and Discipline from 1700 to the Present Day* (New York: St. Martin's, 1990).

2. Richard V. Ericson and Kevin D. Haggerty, *Policing the Risk Society* (Toronto: University of Toronto Press; Oxford: Oxford University Press, 1997).
3. John Keegan, *A History of Warfare* (New York: Vintage, 1993); Martin L. van Creveld, "Computerized War," in *Technology and War: From 2000 B.C. to the Present,* ed. Martin L. van Creveld (New York: Free Press, 1989), 235–49.
4. E. Mendelsohn, "Science, Scientists, and the Military," in *Science in the Twentieth Century,* ed. J. Krige and D. Pestre (Amsterdam: Harwood, 1997), 175–202; D. Dickson, *The New Politics of Science* (New York: Pantheon, 1984); S. Leslie, *The Cold War and American Science: The Military-Industrial Academic Complex at MIT and Stanford* (New York: Columbia University Press, 1993).
5. Dickson, *The New Politics of Science,* 107.
6. Leslie, *The Cold War and American Science;* D. Kevles, *The Physicists: The History of a Scientific Community in America* (New York: Knopf, 1978).
7. Dickson, *The New Politics of Science.*
8. P. Forman, "Behind Quantum Electronics: National Security as the Basis for Physical Research in the United States, 1940–1960," *Historical Studies in the Physical and Biological Sciences* 18 (1987): 194.
9. Gregory McLauchlan and Gregory Hooks, "Last of the Dinosaurs? Big Weapons, Big Science, and the American State from Hiroshima to the End of the Cold War," *Sociological Quarterly* 36, no. 4 (1995): 754.
10. B. Cohen, "The Computer: A Case Study of Support by Government, Especially the Military, of a New Science and Technology," in *Science, Technology, and the Military,* ed. E. Mendelsohn, M. Smith, and P. Weingart (Dordrecht: Kluwer, 1988), 119–54; T. Roszak, *The Cult of Information* (New York: Pantheon, 1986).
11. M. Tolchin and S. Tolchin, *Selling Our Security* (New York: Penguin, 1992), 164.
12. Charles Hables Gray, *Postmodern War* (New York: Guilford, 1997), 52.
13. M. Klare, "The Pentagon's New Paradigm," in *The Gulf War Reader,* ed. M. Sifry and C. Cerf (New York: Random House, 1991), 466–76.
14. J. Adams, *The Next World War: Computers Are the Weapons and the Front Line Is Everywhere* (London: Hutchinson, 1998).
15. McLauchlan and Hooks, "Last of the Dinosaurs?" 766.
16. Van Creveld, "Computerized War," 242.
17. C. McCutcheon, "Computer-Reliant U.S. Society Faces Growing Risk of 'Information War,'" *Congressional Quarterly* (March 1998): 675–78; John Arquilla and David Ronfeldt, "Cyberwar Is Coming!" *Comparative Strategy* 12 (1993): 141–65.
18. "Clinton Lecture," *Economist,* 15 August 1998, 19.
19. Michel Foucault, *Discipline and Punish: The Birth of the Prison,* trans. Alan Sheridan (New York: Vintage, 1977), 169.
20. See Ericson and Haggerty, *Policing the Risk Society.*
21. Maeve W. McMahon, *The Persistent Prison?* (Toronto: University of Toronto Press, 1992).
22. W. Walsh, "Patrol Officer Arrest Rates: A Study of the Social Organization of Police Work," *Justice Quarterly* 2 (1986): 271–90.
23. Ericson and Haggerty, *Policing the Risk Society;* M. Chatterton, "Managing Paperwork," in *Police Research: Some Future Prospects,* ed. M. Weatheritt (Aldershot, U.K.: Gower, 1989), 107–36; Wesley Skogan, *Disorder and Decline: Crime and the Spiral of Decay in American Neighborhoods* (Berkeley and Los Angeles: University of California Press, 1990).
24. David Garland, " 'Governmentality' and the Problem of Crime: Foucault, Criminology, Sociology," *Theoretical Criminology* 1 (1997): 173–214; Pat O'Malley, "Risk, Power, and Crime Prevention," *Economy and Society* 21, no. 3 (1992): 252–75; Malcolm Feeley and Jonathan Simon, "Actuarial Justice: The Emerging New Criminal Law," in *The Futures of Criminology,* ed. David Nelken (London: Sage, 1994), 173–201.
25. Richard V. Ericson and Clifford Shearing, "The Scientification of Police Work," in *The Knowledge Society,* ed. G. Böhme and Nico Stehr (Dordrecht: Reidel, 1986), 129–59; S. Manwaring-Wright, *The Policing Revolution: Police Technology, Democracy, and Liberty*

in Britain (Brighton: Harvester, 1983); Peter K. Manning, *Symbolic Communication: Signifying Calls and the Police Response* (Cambridge, Mass.: MIT Press, 1988).
26. David Lyon, *The Electronic Eye: The Rise of Surveillance Society* (Minneapolis: University of Minnesota Press, 1994), 111.
27. Dianne Gordon, *The Justice Juggernaut: Fighting Street Crime, Controlling Citizens* (New Brunswick, N.J.: Rutgers University Press, 1990).
28. David Burnham, *Above the Law: Secret Deals, Political Fixes, and Other Misadventures of the U.S. Department of Justice* (New York: Scribner, 1997), 134.
29. Ericson and Haggerty, *Policing the Risk Society.*
30. A. Evans-Pritchard, "Europol Allowed to Keep Files on the Innocent," *Vancouver Sun,* 3 February 1998, A13; James Sheptycki, "Transnational Policing and the Making of a Postmodern State," *British Journal of Criminology* 35, no. 4 (1995): 613–35.
31. Lyon, *The Electronic Eye,* 113.
32. A. Northrop, K. Kraemer, and J. L. King, "Police Use of Computers," *Journal of Criminal Justice* 23, no. 3 (1995): 259–75.
33. Gary T. Marx and Nancy Reichman, "Routinizing the Discovery of Secrets: Computers as Informants," *American Behavioral Scientist* (1984): 423–52.
34. Clive Norris and Gary Armstrong, "Categories of Control: The Social Construction of Suspicion and Intervention in CCTV Systems" (ESRC, 1997), quoted in Stephen Graham, "Spaces of Surveillant Simulation: New Technologies, Digital Representations, and Material Geographies," *Environment and Planning D: Society and Space* 16, no. 4 (1998): 492.
35. Northrop, Kraemer, and King, "Police Use of Computers"; Gordon, *Justice Juggernaut.*
36. Mike Davis, *Ecology of Fear: Los Angeles and the Imagination of Disaster* (New York: Holt, 1998), 381.
37. J. Turow, *Breaking Up America: Advertisers and the New Media Order* (Chicago: University of Chicago Press, 1997).
38. Burnham, *Above the Law,* 164.
39. E. Ratledge and J. Jacoby, *Handbook on Artificial Intelligence and Expert Systems in Law Enforcement* (New York: Greenwood, 1989).
40. National Law Enforcement and Corrections Technology Center, "Be ALERT . . . for the Police Car of the Future," *Tech Beat* (1998): 1.
41. N. Fyfe, "City Watching: Closed Circuit Television Surveillance in Public Spaces," *Area* 28 (1996): 37–46.
42. J. Duffy, *Something to Watch Over Us* (BBC News Online, 1999, cited 4 May).
43. David Bamber, "Surveillance Cameras Will 'Predict Crimes,' " *Telegraph,* 17 July 2000.
44. Davis, *Ecology of Fear,* 367; Clive Walker and Martina McGuinness, "Political Violence and Commercial Victims: High Treason against the Political Economy" (paper presented at the Fifteenth International Symposium on Economic Crime, Cambridge, September 1997).
45. George Friedman and Meredith Friedman, *The Future of War: Power, Technology, and American World Dominance in the Twenty-First Century* (New York: St. Martin's Griffin, 1998), 315.
46. R. Uhlig, "Satellite Offers Spy Pictures by Credit Card," *Ottawa Citizen,* 29 December 1997, A14.
47. H. Hough, *Satellite Surveillance* (Port Townsend, Wash.: Loompanics, 1991), 94.
48. John Fiske, "Surveilling the City: Whiteness, the Black Man, and Democratic Totalitarianism," *Theory, Culture, and Society* 15, no. 2 (1998): 73.
49. Richard Quinney, *Class, State, and Crime,* 2d ed. (New York: Longman, 1980), 133.
50. L. Branscomb, ed., *Empowering Technology: Implementing a U.S. Strategy* (Cambridge, Mass.: MIT Press, 1993).
51. McLauchlan and Hooks, "Last of the Dinosaurs?" 769.
52. Peter Andreas, "The Rise of the American Crimefare State," *World Policy Journal* 14 (1997): 41.
53. National Institute of Justice, *Technology for Community Policing: Conference Report* (Washington, D.C.: U.S. Department of Justice, 1996), 13; Nils Christie, "Suitable Ene-

mies," in *Abolitionism: Towards a Non-Repressive Approach to Crime,* ed. H. Bianchi and R. Van Swaaningen (Amsterdam: Free University Press, 1986), 42–54.

54. National Institute of Justice, *Technology Solutions for Public Safety: Conference Report* (Washington, D.C.: U.S. Department of Justice, 1996).

55. Burnham, *Above the Law,* 138.

56. Burnham, *Above the Law,* 138.

57. Associated Press, "Crime Fighting Goes High-Tech: Military Unveils State-of-the-Art Crime Fighting Lab," *ABCnews.com,* 24 September 1999.

58. National Law Enforcement and Corrections Technology Center, "Another Man's Treasure," *Tech Beat* (Winter 1998): 1.

59. Ericson and Haggerty, *Policing the Risk Society.*

60. Michel De Certeau, *The Practice of Everyday Life,* trans. Steven F. Rendall (Berkeley and Los Angeles: University of California Press, 1984).

61. William Chambliss, "Policing the Ghetto Underclass: The Politics of Law and Law Enforcement," *Social Problems* 41, no. 2 (1994): 177–94.

62. National Institute of Justice, *Law Enforcement Technology for the Twenty-first Century: Conference Report* (Washington, D.C.: U.S. Department of Justice, 1995), 9.

63. Clifford Shearing and Philip Stenning, eds., *Private Policing* (Beverly Hills: Sage, 1985).

64. Paul Virilio and Sylvère Lotringer, *Pure War,* trans. Mark Polizzotti (New York: Semiotext(e), 1997), 30.

Waging a War on Immigrants at the U.S.-Mexico Border

Human Rights Implications

Timothy J. Dunn

A U.S. Marine on a clandestine reconnaissance drug surveillance mission for the U.S. Border Patrol in 1997 shot and killed a teenager herding goats near the U.S.-Mexico border in Redford, Texas. This encounter was fraught with misunderstanding, misperceptions, and gross errors, and it graphically illustrates the dangers to human rights posed by the militarization of domestic law enforcement. The militarization of police has perhaps been taken to its highest level in the border region.

The southwest border is the site of the longest-running manifestation of this trend (over a decade) and the home of the deepest institutional ties between the military and police. The military unit that now coordinates nearly all military support for antidrug efforts in the continental United States, Joint Task Force 6 (JTF-6), is located on the border and has worked extensively with the U.S. Border Patrol, a police unit whose first responsibility is immigration enforcement. This chapter focuses on the collaboration between the military and the Border Patrol and highlights the Redford shooting as an instructive episode in understanding this phenomenon and its implications. The chapter is organized around three main topics: the development of military assistance in border enforcement prior to the Redford shooting, the Redford shooting itself and the role of the military since that time, and the human rights implications of this phenomenon. This study is based on information I have drawn from military documents, military journals, border region press, congressional documents, interviews, and my own observations based on four years of fieldwork in El Paso, Texas.[1]

Some background is in order. The U.S. Border Patrol is the main enforcement arm of the Immigration and Naturalization Service (INS). Its chief mission is the apprehension and prevention of entry of undocumented immigrants. Starting in the latter 1980s its formal mission gradually expanded to include drug enforcement as a secondary concern. Prior to this, the Border Patrol operated largely on its own in isolation from other organizations, as it was the sole federal police force focusing on immigration enforcement. However, with the advent of the "war on drugs" in the mid-1980s, and the sharing of drug enforcement duties among a plethora of federal, state, and local organizations, the Border Patrol began to work on a more regular basis with a wide range of other police and military bodies.

It is the collaboration with the U.S. military that raises the most concern, especially from a human rights framework. For over a century before the 1980s, the U.S. military had been largely removed from domestic law enforcement duties. Despite its relevance to public policy and human rights concerns, academics still know relatively little about the topic of Border Patrol–military collaboration, and it has been largely ignored in contemporary studies of immigration and drug issues.

In sum, the purpose of this chapter is to take up this underexamined phenomenon of military support for and collaboration with the Border Patrol. Admittedly, there are other pressing border enforcement matters with profound human rights implications, such as the series of Border Patrol blockades targeting unauthorized immigration that were initiated in key border urban areas during the 1990s.[2] Nonetheless, these types of measures still coincide with a problem-solving approach that revolves around the military model. Moreover, the military's role in border enforcement has serious implications for human rights in and of itself.

Early Military Involvement in Border Enforcement

During the fifteen years leading up to the 20 May 1997 U.S. Marine shooting of Esequiel Hernandez, the military was among the various agencies involved in drug enforcement along the border. The early thrust in drug enforcement at the border mainstreamed the U.S. military into police operations. The military's ability to become directly involved in law enforcement has been limited by a long-standing legal prohibition, the Posse Comitatus statute, which prohibits the military from making arrests, searches, or seizures. However, a series of legal changes starting in 1982, motivated by the emerging drug war, established a whole new chapter in U.S. law allowing the military to provide a vast array of support for civilian police. This includes the provision of military equipment and construction work, military training and transport, and the use of ground troops to assist police. As a means of summarizing the use of militarily allowed and other activities considered by policy makers, I have developed what I term a "spectrum of border militarization" as found in figure 5.1. This spectrum could be applied to examinations of other police-military collaboration cases in the United States, though it was developed based on the border experience.

The newly developed relationship between the military and law enforcement has entailed the establishment of an entirely new set of interorganizational relationships. The Border Patrol has been the primary police unit with whom the military has collaborated.[3] Given that the military had no expertise or experience in regular, nonemergency domestic law enforcement and the criminal justice system, and that its mission and tactics were distinct from that of the Border Patrol, the new relations were tenuous at best. Army Lieutenant General Thomas Kelley, director of operations for the Joint Chiefs of Staff, expressed some of these difficulties in 1989, during the relatively early stages of military-police collaboration:

> We're learning to work with law enforcement agencies, and there's cultural difficulties in doing that and it's a cultural difficulty on our part. When you deal with police officers, they think in terms of going to court and we don't. We're sort of like a special operations soldier who is taught to clear a room by killing the bad guys and not touching the hostages.[4]

The military generally seeks out and destroys an enemy, while law enforcement agencies focus on legal procedure and due process rights. As for the Border Patrol, the bulk of its enforcement encounters are with decidedly nonthreatening immigrants, although a small fraction of their encounters are more dangerous and include some contact with armed drug traffickers.[5]

The military established Joint Task Force 6 in late 1989 at the U.S. Army's Fort Bliss base in El Paso, Texas, with the mission "to serve as a planning and coordinating headquarters to provide support from the De-

Figure 5.1

Spectrum of Militarization of the U.S.-Mexico Border

LESS MILITARISTIC — MORE MILITARISTIC

1	2	3	4	5	6	7	8	9	10	11
Military gives or loans equipment to Border Patrol and law enforcement agencies (BP/LEAs)	Military troops operate or maintain loaned equipment	Military provides "expert advice" to BP/LEAs	Military construction for BP/LEAs	Military provides advisors and training for BP/LEAs	Military transports, supplies, equipment, and personnel for BP/LEAs	Military aerial reconnaissance/ surveillance for BP/LEAs	Military ground troops deployed on small scale at or near border, mainly reconnaissance/ surveillance for BP/LEAs	"Improved integration" or "total integration" of military and BP/LEA efforts. Blurring of institutional lines between military and BP/LEAs	Massive deployment of military troops at or near border to perform a variety of border enforcement roles	Military granted authority to arrest, search, and seize civilians and property

SECTIONS 1–3
Allowed by the 1982 DOD Defense Authorization Law; added new chapter to U.S. law: "Military Cooperation with Civilian Law Enforcement Officials." This support is allowed for police bodies with jurisdiction to enforce drug, contraband, and immigration laws.

SECTIONS 4–9
Allowed by 1989–91 Defense Authorization Laws, amending 1982 provisions, specific to drug enforcement but broader in practice.

SECTIONS 10 AND 11
Bills filed and debated in Congress; no laws passed.

fense Department to federal, state, and local law enforcement agencies." In characterizing the nature of the relations involved in this work, Lieutenant General Stotser, an early commander of JTF-6, stated: "Joint Task Force 6's relationship with law enforcement, in my view, is one of total integration."[6] JTF-6 is mainly an administrative body with a staff of approximately 150 personnel that coordinates military unit support for various police bodies. JTF-6 also put in place a "Rapid Support Unit" made up of Army Special Forces troops to provide an "immediate response to actionable intelligence," some three-quarters of which took the form of ground reconnaissance in 1996.[7] JTF-6's initial geographical focus on the southwest border region was expanded in 1995 to include the entire continental United States.

After nearly a decade, JTF-6 remains one of the longest-lasting joint task forces in U.S. military history, during which more than seventy-two thousand troops have rotated through on temporary missions in thirty states. It still works closely with Operation Alliance, an interagency task force of federal, local, and state law enforcement agencies that coordinates all drug enforcement efforts in the southwest border region. The Border Patrol is a key member of its command structure, along with other federal police bodies. Operation Alliance funnels requests for military assistance from police bodies in the border region. They publicize the availability of military support, screen police requests, help structure the requests so they will pass legal review, and then forward them to JTF-6. JTF-6 lawyers review the police requests and, if approved, post the requests for assistance to the various branches of the military and aid in logistical arrangements.

This police-military collaboration has not always been a straightforward matter. Most notably, telling conflicts emerged in the assault and siege of the Branch Davidians' residence in Waco, Texas. The Waco tragedy involved military support in planning, providing military advisors, and loaning heavy equipment. JTF-6 coordinated the collaboration and had originally authorized a much more expansive list of support, until the Army Special Forces units resisted their recommended level of involvement. JTF-6's original request was pared back, much to the displeasure of overeager JTF-6 officials.[8]

Military Support for the Border Patrol

JTF-6 carried out 1,260 missions from 1990 through 1993, with the majority of those being conducted for the Border Patrol. This makes for an average of 315 missions per year, of which approximately 157 were for the Border Patrol. While precise data are not available for the subsequent years, it was reported that JTF-6 had conducted over 3,300 missions from 1990 through mid-1997.[9] This means more than 2,000 were conducted from 1994 through mid-1997, an average of 571 per year. And while the total number of JTF-6 missions increased dramatically, those involving the Border Patrol grew more modestly, to approximately 171 per year. In other words, the Border Patrol's share dropped to 30 percent after JTF-6 expanded its focus beyond the border to the continental United States in 1995. Thus, while JTF-6 expanded its area of operation and mission total in the mid-1990s, the Border Patrol still received on the whole more JTF-6 support missions than any other single police agency up to the 1997 Redford shooting, certainly more than any other in the southwest border region.

JTF-6 provided law enforcement agencies with nineteen different types of support missions, classified in three broad categories: operational, engineering, and general support. These include construction projects, the deployment of ground troops for various forms of reconnaissance (basically covert surveillance), the loaning of equipment, military training, and intelligence support. This breadth is reflected in the spectrum of border militarization (see fig. 5.1).

Most JTF-6 missions for the Border Patrol fell toward the more militaristic end of the spectrum. For example, in 1997 a JTF-6 official reported that the Border Patrol received most of JTF-6's missions within the broader "operational" category. Most of the missions in that category involve the deployment of ground troops for surveillance or patrol. The most frequently performed type of JTF-6 mission carried out for the Border Patrol was the Listening Post/Observation Post (LP/OP) mission. This is where small groups of soldiers are deployed in remote areas at or near the border to conduct covert surveillance of a suspected drug trafficking area, followed in frequency by electronic ground sensor missions. The number of these LP/OP missions has increased in recent years, from an average of 41 per year for the 1990–93 period to an average of 117 per year between 1994 and mid-1997.[10]

The San Diego County border area was a primary focal point in 1996 for military operations, apparently aiding immigration more than drug enforcement. Some forty-two hundred marines and Green Beret (U.S. Army Special Forces) troops rotated in small teams through a secret operations base, run by the California National Guard, on temporary border drug reconnaissance missions.[11] A JTF-6 source admitted that the San Diego Border Patrol sector had "no counterdrug program in place."[12] The area is well known as a busy undocumented immigration site.

In addition to "operational support," JTF-6 also provides two other types of support to the Border Patrol. The first of these is engineering support, such as the construction of thin, corrugated steel walls along the border at various points, and road construction. Such construction efforts are the most publicly visible type of military support, though it accounts for only 10 percent of all JTF-6 missions. In addition, JTF-6 provides "general support" to the Border Patrol, the two most common forms being intelligence analysis assistance and military team training for Border Patrol officers. These two forms of general support span a broad range, with some being quite militaristic, such as training in small-unit tactics, weapons training, interview and interrogation techniques, use of pyrotechnics, booby trap techniques, and reconnaissance operations. Other forms of support revolve around intelligence gathering and processing, again some with decidedly militaristic overtones, including "target selection" and "intelligence preparation of the battlefield."

Clearly, much of the drug law enforcement assistance provided by the military aids the Border Patrol in its immigration enforcement duties.[13] "Planning experts" from the Pentagon's Center for the Study of Low Intensity Conflict helped design the *Border Patrol Strategic Plan: 1994 and Beyond*.[14] This document is devoted mainly to immigration enforcement and casts both immigration and drug problems as threats to "national security."

In the mid-1990s, as the immigration issue gained prominence, policy makers explicitly directed the military to aid immigration enforcement along the southwest border, thereby surpassing the already established, but more subtle, "spill-over" of military support. The Clinton administration breached an important rhetorical firewall in January 1996, when high-ranking officials announced that 350 military troops would help with immigration enforcement along the border in Arizona and California for the first quarter of the year.[15] This was the first time that high-ranking presidential administration representatives had publicly acknowledged that the military would be used specifically to aid the INS and Border Patrol in immigration enforcement.

The Redford Shooting Incident

A tragic consequence of this trend has come to serve as a lightning-rod example of its potential dangers. On 20 May 1997 Marine Corporal Clemente

Banuelos shot and killed eighteen-year-old Esequiel Hernandez Jr. on the edge of the rural border village of Redford, Texas, during a JTF-6 LP/OP mission looking for drug traffickers along the Rio Grande. Hernandez was completely uninvolved with the drug trade and was only a local high school student known by local residents as a "good kid."[16] This was the first time that soldiers on a border region drug enforcement mission shot and killed a U.S. citizen, though it was at least the fourth shooting by soldiers on such missions.[17] At least one of those resulted in injury, when a January 1997 incident near Brownsville, Texas, left one undocumented immigrant wounded by an Army Special Forces soldier.[18]

Hernandez was killed while herding his goats in the late afternoon near the Rio Grande not far from his house; he was carrying a seventy-year-old, single-shot .22-caliber rifle, which he used to protect his goats from predators. A four-member team of marines on an LP/OP mission for the Border Patrol alleged that he shot at them twice near the river from a distance of approximately 220 yards just after 6 P.M. The soldiers were dressed in full camouflage and moving discreetly through the brush on the way to their observation site for the coming evening. It is not clear that Hernandez knew who or what he was looking at in the brush—but it is unlikely that he knew they were U.S. soldiers.[19]

After Hernandez fired two shots at or near the marine team, they became agitated and radioed their mission commanders to report the episode. Shortly thereafter they contacted the command center, stating, "As soon as he readies that rifle back down range, we are taking him down." The marine radio operator responded to Banuelos, "Roger. Fire back," thus authorizing Banuelos to shoot Hernandez if he pointed his rifle in the team's vicinity.[20]

The mission's commanding officer and other supervisors felt that the authorization to fire was incorrect, but they did not issue any correction and instead replaced the radio operator. A new operator issued a bland warning to "follow the R.O.E. [rules of engagement]," to which Banuelos did not reply. The rules of engagement for this type of mission allow a soldier to fire in self-defense and in defense of others (third parties). However, the officer who briefed the marines on this topic reported that he not only stressed the self-defense and third-party defense criteria but added another: "AND lesser degrees of self-defense had been exhausted."[21] In this case, the latter condition was not met. Banuelos and his team members did not attempt to defuse the incident by identifying themselves, explaining their presence, telling Hernandez to stop shooting at them, or even firing a warning shot.

The soldiers had little preparation for civilian contact, which they were supposed to avoid on the clandestine surveillance mission. The mission commander had told his team leader that in the event of civilian contact they were to "make immediate *force protection* decisions" [italics added] and radio mission command for instructions. Another marine team leader on the same mission recalled later, however, that he had been instructed in the event of civilian contact to identify himself as a marine and ask civilians to leave the area. Banuelos's subsequent actions did not include the latter, but rather an exaggerated sense of the former notion: "force protection."

Hernandez moved away from the river and headed back toward the village; the marine team fanned out and followed him for twenty minutes, though JTF-6 officials maintain the marines "paralleled" him.[22] This seems to violate one of the JTF-6 "rules of engagement" for such missions, which allows soldiers to "pursue armed persons only to defend or retrieve personnel."[23] Although these conditions were not met in this case, the marines felt they were not following him but rather protecting their right flank. Law enforcement officials later recreated the incident and questioned this interpretation.

After following Hernandez for over twenty minutes, the marines claim that Hernandez raised his rifle to fire for a third time and Banuelos shot him in his right side from approximately 140 yards. Hernandez fell and died within sight of his house. Banuelos claimed that he was trying to protect another team member, similarly distanced from Hernandez as himself, in the direction of whom he alleges Hernandez had pointed his rifle.

There are a number of inconsistencies and problems with this version of events. First of all, Banuelos is the only eyewitness to Hernandez's alleged raising of his rifle; the other three marine team members initially told investigators that they did not or could not see Hernandez at that moment, although one changed his statement. The next day, however, after a walk-through re-creation of the episode, a military investigator determined that this same soldier's view was obstructed from his reported position and that he could not have seen Hernandez.

We do know that Banuelos thought he had taken down a "bad guy." He stated, "I capped the [expletive]."[24] Hernandez died as a result of the single shot by Banuelos. The marine team did not render aid to Hernandez, despite the presence of a combat aidsman (trained in combat first aid) on their team. Instead, they let the young man bleed to death; they also failed to call for medical assistance, despite a helicopter medevac unit in nearby Presidio.

The Aftermath of the Redford Shooting

The marine killing of Esequiel Hernandez shook up the border militarization process. For the first time a U.S. Marine faced the prospect of legal prosecution for his actions on a drug support mission. The Pentagon temporarily suspended the use of ground troops along the border, and the marines conducted a lengthy investigation of the incident that brought to light new details about the failures and mishaps surrounding it.

Military officials maintained from the start that the shooting was a "tragic incident" but insisted that the marines had done nothing wrong and that their actions were allowed under the rules of engagement. The military did not cooperate with the investigation by domestic law enforcement authorities, resisting the Texas Rangers' attempts to serve subpoenas for the marines and quickly moving the marines out of state back to their California base. A grand jury acting under state law met twice in Marfa, Texas, before deciding in mid-August 1997 not to indict any of the marines. The grand jury makeup may have compromised its impartiality, as it contained three people with strong ties to the local Border Patrol (including a supervisor who requested the military support in the first place). Two subsequent grand juries were convened in West Texas, one federal and another state; they also failed to indict any of the marines involved.[25] In 1998 the federal government settled a civil wrongful death lawsuit filed by the Hernandez family by paying an unusually large sum of $1.9 million. It admitted no wrongdoing.[26]

At the end of July 1997, just two days before the first grand jury meeting, the Pentagon announced with great fanfare that it was suspending the use of ground troops along the border pending an internal Pentagon review of the practice. In addition, Pentagon officials announced that they would be reviewing ways to protect soldiers who followed the military "rules of engagement" from facing prosecution in civilian courts of law.

Distinct from these legal and policy maneuvers, the most revealing aspect of the aftermath of the Redford shooting was the release in July 1998 of a lengthy, detailed marine internal investigation of the incident that was quite sober and critical. This report shed heretofore unheard-of public light on both the ill-fated mission and marine approaches to these types of missions more generally.[27] Most damning was the chief marine investigator's overall evaluation, finding "systemic failures at every level of command responsible for training, support, and the exercise of command and control" of the Redford mission. In sum, the internal marine investigation showed:

1990 The marines' mission preparation was exceptionally poor and brief.

1991 The marines tended not to take border counterdrug missions very seriously.

1992 JTF-6 (and to a lesser degree the Border Patrol) provided extremely poor, superficial, incomplete, and in part inflammatory and inaccurate orientation and intelligence briefings for the marines.

1993 There was a distinct lack of mission oversight from JTF-6 and marine officials.

These flaws were especially disturbing because the same problems of grossly inadequate marine preparation, support, and oversight were cited in an earlier investigation. All of these problems were supposed to have been corrected by new division policies, but implementation of those was more than lacking.

Border Militarization since the Redford Shooting

In early 1999 the military's new policy on ground troops was that they may be deployed only with the "specific permission of the secretary of defense or his deputy," the purpose of which, according to a military official, "is . . . to ensure . . . the appropriate level of oversight."[28] The decision on returning to the use of ground troops is now left to internal bureaucratic discretion. A recent press report indicates that as of September 2000 the Pentagon had not resumed border deployment of armed ground troops, though they remain an option.[29] Meanwhile, the same report noted that JTF-6 has continued to coordinate all manner of other forms of military support for the Border Patrol, from aerial surveillance by army helicopter units to construction and military intelligence support. The army aerial surveillance missions appear to be quite militaristic; one army commander characterized these operations as "full battle drill" (even though the helicopters were unarmed). In contrast, the relatively less militaristic activities of road and fence building were the most visible military activities for the Border Patrol in West Texas, in the same county as Redford, and in southern New Mexico during the first two years after the Redford shooting.[30]

An August 2000 list of military support missions noted forty-two types available to the police. Those changes relating to the Pentagon's new policy requiring high-level permission for the use of ground troops included an asterisk (*), denoting those mission types using ground troops.[31] This hardly seems like a profound change. In addition, the same source reported that as of August 2000 JTF-6 conducted a total of more than 4,300 missions during its tenure. This makes for about 1,000 additional missions conducted since mid-1997, or some 333 per year on average. Of course, these JTF-6 missions are still conducted throughout the continental United States and not just the border region. Nonetheless, the Border Patrol appears to retain a strong level of support from the unit and a privileged relationship with it.

Given JTF-6's continued influential role, it seems plausible that the military will be involved in future moves to militarize the criminal justice system. Unfortunately, the public is unlikely to be made aware, since JTF-6 has no requirement for regular, public reporting of its activities. Indeed, one JTF-6 official claimed this was "sensitive information" that generally would not be revealed.[32]

Despite the military's reining in of the use of ground troops along the border, it is important to reiterate that the decision of whether or not to resume them is a matter of bureaucratic discretion, not public discussion or debate. If political winds shift over time, the Pentagon's current reticence to deploy ground troops along the border may lessen, and no notification of the public or others outside the Pentagon would be required. Meanwhile, state National Guard troops are exempt from this limited restriction policy, as they fall under state governors' authority, not the Pentagon's. Consequently, armed National Guard ground troops can be used along the border with a governor's approval, a role they have taken up avidly in the past.

The U.S. House of Representatives has considered broadening the use of military troops for drug, terrorist, and immigration enforcement as a means to shore up "national security." In 1997, in 1998, and again in 1999, a bill promoted by Congressman James Traficant (Dem.-Ohio) calling for such has overwhelmingly passed in the House of Representatives. The Defense and Justice Departments have both opposed the measure; however, the Senate has never considered the matter.

A spate of recent articles in two leading U.S. Army journals indicates that some in the military also foresee an expansion of its involvement in domestic law enforcement in the future, particularly at the border and also specifically through JTF-6. One military author, discussing "support to domestic civil authorities during domestic emergencies," states, "These activities also include border-control operations directed against illegal immigration."[33] This support would entail close collaboration with the Border Patrol. Another military author proposes, "Security along the US-Mexico border will become a prominent and growing focus of United States strategic planning . . . [and] military actions."[34] Speculating on likely future U.S.

security problems, the same author and two military colleagues list "illegal immigration and threats to the integrity of national borders" in their top five.[35] Meanwhile, a military lawyer with the U.S. Special Operations Command assumes that "the coming years will see a continuation, if not increase in the employment of the Army within the United States," and specifically to assist civilian law enforcement, under the rubric of which he features JTF-6 most prominently.[36] Although the debate over military involvement in domestic policing is far from concluded within the military or outside it, it is noteworthy that in the U.S. Army's leading journals during recent years the dissenting position against such has been nearly entirely invisible.

Conclusion: Human Rights Implications

Military collaboration with the Border Patrol in the U.S.-Mexico border region on drug and immigration enforcement has been extensive, spanning the past decade. The military has also broadened its geographic focus beyond the border and now has worked with a plethora of other police bodies throughout the United States on drug enforcement. There are signs that military support for border policing may even expand in the future. The human rights implications of this are significant.

What is the significance of human rights for nation-state conduct in general? Bryan Turner observes: "The point about the concept of *human* rights is that they are extra governmental and have traditionally been used to counteract the repressive capacity of states" (italics in original). He further proposes that institutions are often responsible for human rights violations, an outcome he attributes in part to the bureaucratization process.[37] This raises the issue of the relationship between bureaucracy and human rights. Sjoberg and Vaughan propose that bureaucracy tends to undermine the human rights of the "truly disadvantaged" through a process of "social triage" that includes both the sacrifice of their general well-being and dignity as well as the use of stark repression on some occasions. It becomes more "efficient" to write off the rights and well-being of the most subordinated groups, because to address their needs in earnest would entail profound societal reforms and "sacrifices" on the part of elites.[38]

These social theorists have a concern for the rights, dignity, and well-being of people, especially subordinated groups. The primary threat to these groups are institutions and bureaucratic power structures. The efforts of the Border Patrol and military are directed against especially subordinated groups, such as working-poor undocumented immigrants and often poor, low-level drug couriers (so-called mules). In the border region this generally means those of Hispanic appearance, especially Mexicans and Mexican Americans. Based on the previous concepts, the human rights of members of those groups would be the most likely to be "sacrificed" for the goal of increased border enforcement. This has definitely been the pattern in the Border Patrol's troubled human rights record in the region.[39]

While the military has had relatively little public contact generally, it is responsible for one of the most severe human rights abuses arising so far from border enforcement, namely, the marine killing of a U.S. citizen, a Mexican American teenager in Redford, Texas. The use of the military along the border led to gross misunderstandings by soldiers and their unwarranted escalation in the use of force, rather than the deescalation of or retreat from a tense, unclear situation in the field. This illustrates the danger of the inappropriate matching of military troops against nonmilitary threats (indeed, social problems, not threats) bound up in border enforcement. As Lawrence Korb, a former assistant secretary of defense in the Reagan administration, stated shortly after the Redford incident, "The military, to put it bluntly, is trained to vaporize, not Mirandize."[40] It is consistent with the human rights concepts raised earlier that this human rights violation against a young minority group member was incurred as a part of a mistake-filled collaboration between two powerful, coercive state bureaucracies.

Even less severe forms of military collaboration in border policing have negative implications for the status of human rights. For instance, much of the military training and intelligence support offered by JTF-6 seems entirely inappropriate for civilian police bodies. Military interrogation techniques and military raids, for example, and military intelligence activities, in general, are typically not designed or conducted with concern for the U.S. legal system's requirements for safeguarding suspects' rights, but rather with the elimination or neutralization of an enemy threat.

Another danger is that while drug law enforcement militarization was once focused on the southwest border region, it has subsequently spread to interior areas. In that vein, the spectrum of border militarization that I developed (fig. 5.1) could be used to examine its internal development, for the border experience appears to be a vanguard of a larger process of military-police collaboration being extended elsewhere throughout the United States. Although the use of ground troops is restricted mainly to border areas, other types of military support for police agencies around the country, such as training in military operational and intelligence tactics, could lead police to adopt ever more military tactics in their operations (see chapter 6). Blurring the lines between the police and the military has long been associated with human rights problems.

The U.S.-Mexico border has served as a contemporary proving ground for the militarization of law enforcement: it has been implemented largely out of public view against subordinate groups in this peripheral region on a broader scale than anywhere else within the United States during the contemporary era. This represents an insidious form of military "mission creep" and an expansion of militarism that is not wholly inconsistent with the state's punitive efforts to wage intensified wars against crime and drugs. This collaboration between the state's main corporal bureaucratic power structures does not bode well for the vulnerable status of subordinated groups. Policy makers have hardly considered this concern for human rights; continuing that neglect will likely be a grave error given the intrinsic importance of human rights as a building block for a decent, democratic society. The security of our human rights may hang in the balance.

Notes

This chapter is a revised version of "Military Collaboration with the Border Patrol in the U.S.-Mexico Region," *Journal of Political and Military Sociology* 27, no. 2 (1999): 257–78.

1. I would like to thank Jose Palafox, Joe Nevis, Peter Andreas, Jean-Paul Hanon, Doug Holt, Monty Paulsen, and Derrick Starr for sharing with me some key research materials I draw upon in this study. I would also like to thank Amy Liebman for various supports, especially key editorial assistance in completing this chapter.
2. The Border Patrol blockades and other immigration enforcement efforts have had profound human rights consequences, such as an estimated sixteen hundred accidental border-crossing deaths from 1993 to 1997 and more than five hundred such deaths from 1994 to 2000 in the California-Mexico border area alone; Karl Escbach, Jaqueline Hagan, Nestor Rodriguez, Rubon Hernandez Leon, and Stanley Bailey, "Death at the Border," *International Migration Review* 33, no. 2 (1999): 430–54; American Friends Service Committee, personal communication, 25 August 2000. These have been largely the result of migrants attempting to make unauthorized crossings while avoiding the Border Patrol, whose blockades have increasingly forced crossers to more remote and dangerous areas.
3. Interview with anonymous official of Joint Task Force 6, 30 April 1997.
4. House Committee on the Armed Services, *Narcotics Interdiction and the Use of the Military* (Washington, D.C.: U.S. Government Printing Office, 1989).
5. Field notes from Border Patrol Citizens Academy class, 18 October 1995. I participated in a six-session "Border Patrol Citizens Academy" offered by the El Paso Border Patrol in the fall of 1995, which consisted of a series of talks by Border Patrol agents on a variety of topics. The BPCA is a public relations/outreach effort of the local Border Patrol to educate members of the public on its mission and activities and, as we were told, to encourage us "to see our job from our perspective." The speakers made quite clear that most of the people they apprehend are undocumented immigrants who are for the most part

quite nonthreatening and well behaved. I have been told similar things by agents for years before and since in El Paso and elsewhere.

6. Both quotes are from a Pentagon statement quoted in a 1989 press report cited in Timothy J. Dunn, *The Militarization of the U.S.-Mexico Border, 1978–1992: Low Intensity Conflict Doctrine Comes Home* (Austin: University of Texas at Austin Center for Mexican American Studies Books, 1996), 134.

7. William W. Mendel and Murl D. Munger, "The Drug Threat: Getting Priorities Straight," *Parameters: U.S. Army War College Quarterly* 27, no. 2 (1997): 116.

8. Thomas R. Lujan, "Legal Aspects of Domestic Employment of the Army," *Parameters: U.S. Army War College Quarterly* 27, no. 3 (1997): 4 (of on-line version).

9. Douglas Holt, "DA Questions Military Account of Border Slaying," *Dallas Morning News,* 4 June 1997.

10. These LP/OP mission averages are based on figures for 1990–93 drawn from U.S. Army Corps of Engineers, *Programmatic Environmental Impact Statement: JTF-6 Activities along the U.S.-Mexico Border* (April 1994), 4-2 draft copy, as cited in Dunn, *Militarization of the U.S.-Mexico Border,* 135, compared with the figures for the period from 1990 through mid-1997 reported in Larry Lee, "Border Soldiers Get More Lessons in Deadly Force," *El Paso Herald-Post,* 3 July 1997, and Holt, "DA Questions Military Account of Border Slaying."

11. H. G. Reza, "Patrols Border on Danger," *Los Angeles Times,* 29 June 1997.

12. "After Action Report, Counterdrug Mission . . . U.S. Border Patrol, San Diego, CA," unpublished document by anonymous military intelligence official, 17 March 1997, 9.

13. Interviews with an anonymous JTF-6 official, 30 April 1997, and with another anonymous JTF-6 official, 15 August 1995.

14. U.S. Border Patrol, *Border Patrol Strategic Plan: 1994 and Beyond, National Strategy* (1994), 1–2.

15. Patrick McDonnell and Sebastian Rotella, "Military, Police to Aid in New Push by Border Patrol," *Los Angeles Times,* 12 January 1996.

16. Douglas Holt, "Top Border Official Calls Fatal Shooting 'Tragic,' " *Dallas Morning News,* 23 May 1997.

17. Lee, "Border Soldiers Get Lesson in Deadly Force"; John T. Coyne, "Investigation to Inquire into the Circumstances Surrounding the Joint Task Force-6 (JTF-6) Shooting Incident That Occurred on 20 May 1997 Near the Border between the United States and Mexico," unpublished report (1998), 13, 136.

18. Thaddeus Herrick, "Two Cases This Year Raise Questions about Military's Role on Rio Grande," *Houston Chronicle,* 22 June 1997.

19. Barbara Ferry, "Looking for the Border," *Texas Observer,* 18 July 1997.

20. Both quotes from Coyne, "Investigation to Inquire," 68.

21. Quoted in Coyne, "Investigation to Inquire," 38–39.

22. Ferry, "Looking for the Border."

23. Laura Smitherman, "Opposition to Military on Border Grows," *El Paso Times,* 13 July 1997; Coyne, "Investigation to Inquire," 38–39.

24. Douglas Holt, "Border Inquiry Falls to Other Investigators: End of Congressional Probe Alters Status," *Dallas Morning News,* 18 September 1997; Monty Paulsen, "Drug War Masquerade," *San Antonio Current,* 8 September 1998.

25. Associated Press, "Shooting Death Won't Bring Civil Rights Charges," *El Paso Times,* 27 February 1998; Richard Estrada, "Death Payoff Won't Fix Border Patrol Policy," *Dallas Morning News,* 8 August 1998.

26. Eduardo Montes, "U.S. Pays Family of Teen Shot on Border," *El Paso Times,* 12 August 1998.

27. Coyne, "Investigation to Inquire"; for excellent press summaries see Douglas Holt, "An Identity Crisis Most Deadly," *Chicago Tribune,* 5 July 1998, and Paulsen, "Drug War Masquerade." The investigation report by Marine Corps Major General John T. Coyne is the only available summary of the vast quantity of information gathered in the course of a host of official investigations, totaling some thirteen thousand pages, from the Marine Corps's inquiry to various federal and state criminal investigations as well as earlier mili-

tary inquiries. Most of the relevant information on the incident itself basically corroborates what was previously reported in the media in the immediate aftermath of the event, as cited previously.

28. Douglas Holt, "Pentagon Ends Routine Use of Troops along Mexican Border," *El Paso Times,* 28 January 1999.

29. Mike Glenn, "Laredo Patrol Welcomes Military, but Some Residents Say It's Too Much," *Houston Chronicle,* 2 September 2000.

30. Field notes, May 1998, April 1999.

31. JTF-6 website (http://www.jtf6.bliss.army.mil). Most of the increase from nineteen to forty-two types of support (in comparing this document to earlier ones) is that a number of training and intelligence support activities have now been specified.

32. Field notes, conversation with JTF-6 official, 15 September 1998.

33. Kevin Stringer, "A Homeland Defense Mission," *Military Review* 80, no. 3 (2000): 98.

34. Graham H. Turbiville Jr., "U.S.-Mexican Border Security: Civil-Military Cooperation," *Military Review* 79, no. 3 (1999): 37–38.

35. Graham H. Turbiville Jr., William W. Mendel, and Jacob W. Kipp, "The Changing Security Environment," *Military Review* 77, no. 3 (1997): 3–4 (on-line version). The other four of their top-five list of security problems were insurgencies and separatist movements; heavily armed criminal gangs and paramilitaries; arms trafficking and illegal trade in strategic materials; and a broad one encompassing disasters, environmental damage, and public health threats. Lest we think this is fringe thinking in military circles, it seems significant that this is from the lead article in an entire issue of *Military Review* (May–June 1997) devoted to "Security Challenges and the Nature of the Future War." *Military Review* is the journal of the U.S. Army Command and General Staff College.

36. Lujan, "Legal Aspects of Domestic Employment of the Army," 1, 3–5 of on-line version.

37. Bryan S. Turner, "Outline of a Theory of Human Rights," in *Citizenship and Social Theory,* ed. B. Turner (London: Sage, 1993), 178, 182.

38. Gideon Sjoberg and Ted R. Vaughan, "The Ethical Foundations of Sociology and the Necessity for a Human Rights Alternative," in *A Critique of Contemporary American Sociology,* ed. Ted R. Vaughan, Gideon Sjoberg, and Larry Reynolds (Dix Hills, N.Y.: General Hall, 1993), 114–59; Gideon Sjoberg, "The Human Rights Challenge to Communitarianism: Formal Organization and Race and Ethnicity," in *Macro Socio-Economics,* ed. David Sciulli (Armonk, N.Y.: Sharpe, 1996), 273–97.

39. See Human Rights Watch/Americas, *United States Crossing the Line: Human Rights Violations along the U.S. Border with Mexico Persist amid Climate of Impunity* (New York: Human Rights Watch/Americas, April 1995); Immigration Law Enforcement Monitoring Project, American Friends Service Committee, *Sealing Our Borders: The Human Toll, Third Annual Report* (Philadelphia: American Friends Service Committee, 1992); Dunn, *Militarization of the U.S.-Mexico Border,* 93–94; Timothy J. Dunn, "Immigration Enforcement in the U.S. Mexico Border Region, the El Paso Case: Bureaucratic Power, Human Rights, and Civic Activism," Ph.D. diss. (University of Texas at Austin, 1999); Timothy J. Dunn, "Border Enforcement and Human Rights Violations in the Southwest," in *Race and Ethnic Relations in the United States: Readings for the Twenty-first Century,* ed. Chris Ellison and W. Alan Martin (Los Angeles: Roxbury, 1999).

40. Holt, "DA Questions Military Account of Border Slaying."

Community Policing in Battle Garb

A Paradox or Coherent Strategy?

Matthew T. DeMichele
Peter B. Kraska

An emerging body of crime and justice scholarship studies recent macro-level changes in criminal justice practices that are incoherent, contradictory, and volatile. Most attempts to make theoretical sense of these contrasting changes come out of penology, the study of punishment and corrections.[1] For example, David Garland, a leading penological scholar, argues that these changes are a signal that the state is no longer able to control crime. He theorizes that as the criminal justice system reaches its capacity to lower crime rates, governments enact divergent and contradictory policies, characterized by programs that emphasize prevention and forming partnerships versus those that stress "enhanced control and expressive punishment."[2] Simon, for his part, offers a rather different explanation for this heterogeneity in criminal justice policy. According to Simon, penal modernity as a uniform model has reached its "end game."[3] As we fold into an era of postmodernity, the traditional guides to punishment, such as rehabilitation, no longer steer policy and practice in any sort of coherent fashion.

The purpose of this chapter is to make sense of a similar sort of incoherence characterizing not corrections but instead the police, specifically community-oriented versus paramilitary policing. While penological scholars have been theorizing the emergence of polar discourses and practices within correctional policy, the study of police has yet to offer such analytical insights. Rather, police studies, for nearly two decades, have been trained toward advocating and evaluating community policing reforms in search of an answer to the bureaucratic question, "What works?" This type of advocacy scholarship, while providing important evaluations of new police practices, has left discussions of major changes affecting contemporary policing undeveloped.

As a result, police studies have not adequately addressed or explained the emergence of both community policing reforms and an array of controversial practices that seem to run counter to the idea of community policing. For example, little academic research or discussion has been devoted to the proliferation of civil asset forfeiture procedures, the expansion of warrantless searches into public housing developments, the deployment of sophisticated surveillance systems, the rapid movement toward policing schools, a host of aggressive tactics characterized as zero tolerance, and the rise and normalization of police paramilitary units (PPUs or SWAT teams).[4]

The last two developments listed, zero-tolerance policies and the rise of paramilitary policing, are of particular importance. As police scholars concentrate on community policing's democratic reforms, the real world of policing has experienced a more complex program of change, including the growth and normalization of police paramilitary units. It may seem ironic to discuss aggressive, militaristic sorts of policing in conjunction with community policing reforms. However, ethnographic fieldwork and two national surveys demonstrate that the PPU approach to policing has a strong presence in self proclaimed community policing–oriented departments.

This chapter seeks to confront and make sense of the emergence of two contrasting visions in contemporary policing—one based on a democratic model, the other on a military model. We start out by briefly examining the community and paramilitary policing models, focusing on their dominant themes. We then employ the latest penological literature on developments in social control to place these apparently contradictory phenomena in their larger structural context. While this literature sheds considerable light on this phenomenon, our final analysis questions the commonsense interpretation that community and paramilitary policing are necessarily antithetical. On close inspection, the simultaneous emergence of these approaches does not necessarily signal an incongruity stemming from a state in crisis.[5] To the contrary, when examining the real-world application of these differing approaches, they exhibit what Rose terms a "strategic coherence."

Developing Strands of Community Policing

The concept of community policing is renowned for its ambiguity, making clear definitions or generalizations nearly impossible. Our limited objective is to sketch briefly the dominant themes of two different strands of community policing. For the purposes of this discussion, one version of community policing will be referred to as "zero tolerance" or "order maintenance," and the other as "peace-corps policing" (with an emphasis on citizen empowerment, peacekeeping, and community building). Dividing community policing into two strands is not meant to imply that all police agencies follow either one approach or the other. Our objective instead is to demonstrate that the community policing reform agenda as a whole contains within it differing assumptions and prescriptions aligned with differing ideologies. Before discussing either strand, however, a brief review of community policing's precursors is needed to demonstrate the origins and preconditions that make community policing socially and politically viable.[6]

Police scholars, public officials, and citizens all praise community policing as an innovative and effective approach uniting the police and citizens in a mutual effort against crime and disorder. Community policing reformers wanted to change the "we/they" attitude inherent in the preceding rational-legalistic professional model. The professional policing model emphasized centralized authority, hierarchical structure, and bureaucratic rationality. Professional police administrators relied on numerical representations of performance, most notably crime statistics and response time, to evaluate officers.[7]

Police officers in the professional model, epitomizing the military-bureaucratic philosophy, were to patrol their assigned areas (beats), look for any law violations, and make arrests. They were not to intervene in any non-criminal matters, only those that offended the criminal code; police rationally reacted to criminal situations. In accordance with this rational-legalistic emphasis, police officers were ostensibly held accountable for their daily activities.

The move to this bureaucratic model is attributed to the rampant corruption and poor supervision of police during the late nineteenth and early twentieth centuries. The police had a close relationship with local political regimes and the people they were to police. Administrative control was sorely lacking. Decentralization and close political relationships removed any possibility for supervising daily police functions, thus granting officers nearly complete discretion and leading to widespread abuse of power.

The gross politicization of the police (and all other governmental agencies) during this time led reformers to devise strategies to distance the police from politicians. Reducing corruption involved removing patronage (political favoritism, nepotism) from the police institution and reformulating the recruitment, selection, training, and retention of police officers.[8] The professional model shifted police authority from local politics to the rule of law and professional edicts.

These rational managerial schemes, however, were not as effective for the police as they had been for American business. The police institution made minimal gains in legitimating themselves with the public they served, and their efforts did not positively affect the crime rate. The inability to decrease crime discredited the rational-bureaucratic model of policing, especially as administrators became aware of the limited effect of speedy response times and increased police presence. It seemed that the only measurable and positive impact the police could generate was the reduction in citizens' fear of crime. Administrators began to realize that while they can do little to reduce crime, they can manage the image of crime and crime control. Police administrators and other public officials began to focus more on community relations and making people feel safer.

Community policing became a sort of rhetorical panacea for community ills after police administrators and public officials realized that such seemingly effective methods of policing as preventative patrol and efficiency-oriented crime fighting did not reduce crime. Community policing purported to realign police functions to improve citizen satisfaction, reduce fear of crime, and remove the "we/they" attitude epitomized by the military-bureaucratic (professional) model.

Strand One: No Tolerance for Broken Windows

The crux of the first strand of community policing is that crime could be reduced by attending to common disorderly behaviors such as drunkenness, idleness, open-air drug dealing, loitering minorities, homelessness, graffiti artists, peddlers, squeegee men, and so on. This new organizational mandate focused on creating a climate of order in the community by having little tolerance for disorderly behaviors and conditions.[9]

This mandate required the police to get out of their cruisers and take control of their community in order to foster a tighter working relationship with the citizens they served. The "broken windows" thesis, touted by Wilson and Kelling, posited that signs of communal disregard and incivilities demonstrate that no one cares about the community. The incremental decaying of community life resulted in people seizing upon opportunities to commit crimes after rationally calculating the potential gains and losses from such acts.[10] Wilson and Kelling described the process:

> Untended behavior leads to the breakdown of community controls. A stable neighborhood can change, in a few years or even a few months, to an inhospitable and frightening jungle. A piece of property is abandoned, weeds grow up, a window is smashed. Adults stop scolding children; the children, emboldened, become more rowdy. Families move out, unattached adults move in. Teenagers gather in front of the corner store. The merchant asks them to move; they refuse. Fights occur. Litter accumulates. People start drinking in front of the grocery; in time, an inebriate slumps to the sidewalk and is allowed to sleep it off. Pedestrians are approached by panhandlers.[11]

As Wilson and Kelling imply, a healthy community will rapidly deteriorate into a disorganized one as informal social controls (family, church, and schools) weaken. When these informal controls deteriorate, fear of crime increases to the point that many community members hesitate to leave their homes, creating a community characterized by "obstreperous teenagers" that prey upon and frighten the isolated elderly.

Wilson and Kelling led police scholars and public officials to develop methods for the police to govern these disorderly behaviors and the locations in which they occurred. Community policing, therefore, shifted police attention from strict military-bureaucratic administration and centralized organization, concerned with serious crime, to one more interested in reducing criminal opportunities and fostering positive police-citizen relations. By focusing on the broken windows in a location, the police and the community can work together to clean up the community through "linking order-maintenance and crime prevention."[12]

The "broken windows" model, like many theoretical doctrines, made a lot of sense to a lot of people—hence its popularity. As with other common-sense doctrines, however, the real-world application of Wilson and Kelling's approach to community policing has fueled tremendous controversy. It has devolved, in many instances, into a zero-tolerance policing model. Zero-tolerance policing refers to the strict enforcement of all criminal and civil violations within certain geographical hot spots (a code word for lower-income, minority areas) using an array of aggressive tactics such as street sweeps, proactive enforcement of not just the law but "community order," and a proliferation of drug raids on private residences. The best-known example of zero-tolerance community policing developed in the New York City Police Department. This approach, touted as a great success by Mayor Rudolph Giuliani, is being replicated in numerous cities across the country through a model they term COMPSTAT. COMPSTAT relies on strict command and control, zero tolerance for indices of disorder in communities, an aggressive attack on problem areas as determined through sophisticated computer analysis, and a tough system of accountability for supervisors to reduce crime.

Strand Two: Police as Peace Corps

Even though zero-tolerance policing operates in several cities across the United States and abroad, it is not the only community policing model. In fact, while Wilson and Kelling emphasized crime control through aggressively confronting disorder, academics such as Louis Radelet and Robert Trojanowicz were promoting a brand of community policing that emphasized community empowerment, cultivating constructive relationships with disenfranchised minority groups, and establishing partnerships between the public and the police.[13] In this strand of community policing, the end goal is for the community to actively police their own communities.

In contrast to zero-tolerance enforcement, this strand envisions citizens sharing information and creating partnerships with the police and other public and private agencies, so that community problems (only one of which is crime) can be approached more intelligently. Police are better able to aid in community building and to establish community-based problem-solving programs by attending to the social and cultural preconditions that make crime more likely.[14]

This style of policing has been theorized as part of an emerging neoliberal strategy that seeks to reduce state responsibility for safety and security.[15] As the public becomes more aware of the criminal justice system's inability to control crime, this type of community policing attempts to empower, activate, and shift responsibility to the citizenry. It assumes that the police are no longer the sole provider of safety; private citizens and other private entities must participate in policing their own communities.[16]

Each of these contrasting models of community policing contains differing ideological assumptions about the role of police in the community. Wilson and Kelling's zero-tolerance model seeks to "clean up" a community proactively, thereby reducing the potential for crime and diminishing citizens' fears, while the other model is concerned with building responsible and knowledgeable communities through police-citizen partnerships. These two strands of community policing often operate side by side within the same department without an acknowledgment of the inherent ideological differences between the two.

Both models, however, do share key features. These include placing a premium on:

- Proactive policing and crime prevention
- Democratic reforms both within the department and with the community they serve
- Less bureaucratization and enhanced officer freedom
- The establishment of trust between the citizens and the police and a reduction in the fear of crime
- A quest to reclaim the neighborhood through an emphasis on policing places (hot spots), as opposed to pursuing individual law violators

Militarizing the American Police

Now that the foundation of community policing has been discussed, we can briefly sketch the central aspects of another contemporary and seemingly contradictory police development. Indeed, as the correctional field has seen the emergence of incoherent policies and rhetoric, so has the police institution. Specifically, community policing reforms have been accompanied by a proliferation of police paramilitary units in large, medium, and small police departments.[17]

Kraska and Kappeler discovered that between 1980 and 1996, the numbers of PPUs nearly doubled in medium to large cities. This growth was ubiquitous. Small jurisdictions (between twenty-five thousand and fifty thousand citizens) experienced a more marked growth: a 157 percent increase from 1985 to 1995; more than 65 percent of small-town departments have a PPU; and almost two out of every ten police officers in small-town agencies are assigned at least part-time to a PPU.[18]

The increase in PPU activities is even more pronounced. Before the late-1980s drug war, these units were used as high-powered reactive units, typically responding to the rare hostage situation, barricaded suspect, or civil disturbance. This has all changed. Today, about 80 percent of PPU activity is proactive. Specifically, serving search and arrest warrants, most often as no-knock drug raids, accounts for more than three-quarters of all PPU activity.

In addition, about 18 percent of small, medium, and large police departments use their PPU at least periodically to patrol high-crime neighborhoods. The assignment of these normal, everyday police functions to elite paramilitary squads debunks the image of the stereotypical SWAT team as handling mostly hostile terrorists, crazed barricaded gunmen, or other urban legends.[19] Kraska and Kappeler summarize their findings:

> Our research found a sharp rise in the number of police paramilitary units, rapid expansion in their activities, the normalization of paramilitary units into mainstream police work, and a close ideological and material connection between PPUs and the US armed forces.[20]

These units usually comprise ten to thirty-five officers and are modeled directly after military special operations squads such as the Navy Seals or Delta Force. Policing with paramilitary units stresses a centralized organization, tight command structure, regimented training, and military discipline. PPUs operate from an ideology of militarism, which accentuates the use of state force and its accompanying technological tools to solve certain crime and disorder problems—drug possession and dealing behind closed doors, high-crime hot spots, community disorder, civil disturbances, and high-risk situations involving barricaded suspects and hostage taking.

On its face, it might seem inappropriate to discuss community policing reforms and the movement toward militarizing a component of the police together; however, this is what appears to be happening. All the departments surveyed that had an active PPU also claimed to place high emphasis on the democratic approach of community policing. These data, therefore, document the concurrent emergence of two ideologically contradictory police developments. The police institution has simultaneously pursued highly publicized community policing reforms while enacting a less visible transformation based on the military special operations model.

A Punishment and Social Control Context

Thus far we have asserted that the democratic reforms of community policing have emerged alongside a rapid expansion of police paramilitarism. These developments, on their face, are ideologically and operationally incongruent. How do we make sense of this seeming paradox? What social, political, and cultural preconditions best explain this contradiction? A need exists to expand our theoretical gaze.

As noted earlier, correctional scholars have already recognized and theorized similar trends in contemporary practices of punishment. We intend, therefore, to make sense of these recent police developments by extending and synthesizing theoretical approaches offered by several penological scholars. First, we review the "governmentality" approach to viewing social control in society. Second, we examine the reasons given by penologists as to why we have this paradoxical situation. Finally, we use both the governmentality approach and the proposed explanations to help us to understand the paradox between militarization and democratization in policing.

The Governmentality Approach

One axiom of political thought is that governments construct complex programs, technologies, rationalities, and other mechanisms to guide, shape, and steer public thought and action. Indeed, governments have since at least the eighteenth century sought to align the public's sensibilities and activities to those of the dominant political will.[21] While to many, especially those living in "free" democratic societies, this might seem more likely to occur in overpowering socialist regimes, liberal democratic societies also seek to control the citizenry through an assortment of agents, agencies, and institutions, both public and private.[22] In liberal societies, however, the citizenry is afforded a certain level of autonomy and granted civil liberties or rights, not to be violated by the government. This paradox—restraining behavior without offending citizens' rights—has troubled liberal governments since their inception. To confront this paradox, liberal governments have institutionalized several locations (schools, prisons, doctors' offices, and so on) that attempt to implant the needed mind-set (i.e., intellectual or subjective positions) to rule a given population, a mind-set referred to by Foucault as "technologies of the self."[23]

This type of analysis, known in the literature as governmentality studies, helps us to realize that the criminal law is only one mechanism used to order society. In fact, this perspective sees the criminal justice system as playing only a minor role in the complex of control practices. Governments create institutions and experts around vast locales of knowledge that serve to diffuse a government's power or ability to inscribe self-steering mechanisms within individuals in order to govern at a distance.[24] As modernity fostered egalitarianism, proportionality, rationality, and science in society in general, so too were these sentiments included in developing practices of control and punishment. This modern form of control or government sought to align the citizenry less through brute force and disciplines of the body and more through inscribing "technologies of the self" within the majority. This is not to say that bodily forms of punishment ceased, but rather to acknowledge that governments mostly use a complex circuitry of mundane forms of rule to order a given population.

It is the intersections and interactions of a multiplicity of these controls that make possible the maximization of the health, wealth, and morality of a population, and hence the government, of a given territory. These relationships or networks are said to have "governmentalized" the state. In other words, the all-powerful sovereign state loses sway as other, more local centers of power are created (e.g., managers, bureaucrats, teachers, doctors, lawyers, psychiatrists, and other experts of daily life). More importantly, power is defined less as a matter of national territory and more by the government's knowledge of the mass of its population through calculations of births, deaths, diseases, crime, and other areas of control.[25] Liberal governments, therefore, depend on "a whole variety of alliances and lash-ups between diverse and competing bodies of expertise, criteria of judgment and technical devices that are far removed from the political apparatus as traditionally conceived."[26] That is, governments construct many institutions, both state and nonstate, to assist in aligning the aspirations of private individuals with those of the government.[27]

As "good government" entails the coordination of numerous programs in diverse locales, the police institution, similarly, consists of numerous tasks and a variety of discourses and technologies to accomplish those tasks.[28] For this reason, we contend that the police institution makes an excellent site to theorize the criminal justice system with a "governmentality" analysis. The police institution and the criminal justice system in general are merely components of a complex of interconnections and overlappings with various private and public agencies.

As society continues to confront major cultural and political changes (what some call high modernity), these complex intertwinings intensify. One manifestation of this intensification is the previously discussed volatility, ambivalence, and incoherence between its various programs and rationalities. In focusing on trends in punishment, penological scholars see a dislocation in correctional policy and practice characterized by "contradictory couples." These include "disciplinary obedience versus incapacitation, warehousing versus correctional reform, punishment and stigmatization versus reintegration, [and] formal criminalization versus informal victim/offender settlements."[29]

Explaining the Paradox

There has been a good deal of discussion about why exactly this state of incoherence and volatility has emerged. Feeley and Simon emphasize the ascendance of a new statistics-based logic that focuses on managing risks in certain populations; O'Malley asserts that the attempt to combine neoliberal and neoconservative political rationalities accounts for the current state of incoherence; Simon posits that postmodern negativity has replaced more innovative modernist punishments; Garland argues that high crime rates and the criminal justice system's inability to affect them have resulted in a legitimation crisis for governments.[30] A brief explanation of a few of these theories would be helpful.

Feeley and Simon argue that a new language has emerged in contemporary punishment practices. This language shifts the once individualizing and moralizing gaze of legal discourse into one more concerned with actuarial calculations of risk management, not crime reduction. They posit that the dominance of managerial mentalities shifts focus from concerns of legal due process and discovering guilt to a preoccupation with bureaucratic rationality and system efficiency. The focus on system efficiency and rational, pragmatic penal strategies has displaced the progressive agenda of rehabilitation, signaling an emerging postmodern penality. According to this framework, the central governmental objective is to maximize resource allocation and properly *manage risks* of classes of potential offenders.

Feeley and Simon argue that this "new penology" is the effect of significant social and cultural changes. Garland, on the other hand, asserts that "the penal system is only now experiencing a form of management that has long been taken for granted elsewhere."[31] Garland claims that, regardless of the significance of these changes, they should not be considered as signs of a novel sociohistoric transformation. Rather, they are better understood as governmental shifts away from welfare strategies that now stress accountability, auditing, and fiscal controls recognized in other policy sectors.

For Garland, this businesslike ethos is most evident in the devolution of budgets and financial responsibilities as well as the privatization of criminal justice functions (e.g., private police and prisons).[32] Indeed, governments reacted to the many failures of the penal-welfare strategy by embarking on a trend toward downsizing state responsibility for crime control.[33] Governments began incorporating community participation through citizen empowerment programs and civilian empowerment schemes (e.g., community policing). These are all signs of contemporary crime control reaching the limits of the sovereign state. The underlying cause for this governmental response is the normalization of high crime rates in several Western nations. Garland asserts that "high rates of crime have gradually become a taken for granted element of late modern life," prompting a perpetual political ambivalence.[34]

The ambivalence in question is characterized by bipolar crime control strategies—rehabilitation versus retribution or instrumental versus emotive punishments. Governments, in order to face this crime control predicament, have realized the "need to withdraw or at least qualify their claim to be the primary provider of security and crime control."[35] On the one hand, this revelation has fostered the development of pragmatic administrative strategies to improve system functioning (instrumental); on the other hand, this strategy is partnered with a qualitatively different strategy of denying responsibility (passion-driven punishment). Politicians, aware of the consequences of seeming weak or soft on crime, have begun reasserting the state's power to punish through harsh sentences and strict law enforcement.

While Garland contends that the sovereign state has reached its limits to control crime, Pratt and Simon suggest that we are witnessing early indicators of an emerging postmodern penality.[36] They argue that modern punishment has reached its end game. A "new punitiveness" is emerging in the West, suspending individual rights and liberties, the very essence of modern punishment. The new punitiveness is said to reach beyond modernity itself, employing tactics and retributive and even militaristic schemes (see chapter 7) that are more reflective of a premodern or nonmodern punishment. Simon and Pratt argue that these noble modernist goals have been replaced by distorted representational images of proper social order and security in which reason has given way to emotion.[37]

Contemporary Punishment Studies Applied to Policing

By employing a governmentality framework and the explanations provided as to why this state of incoherence and volatility has arisen in the area of punishment, we can see today's police institution in a much clearer light. Earlier we discussed, for example, the development of numerous controversial police tactics in the war against crime and drugs (no-knock contraband raids, racial profiling, civil asset forfeiture, street sweeps, etc.). These divisive, emotive, and repressive tactics are unfolding alongside community policing reforms that call for helping communities and improving their quality of life. For both Garland and Simon, this incoherence signals that the sovereign state is in crisis. The state is attempting to reassert its traditional power while adapting to large-scale cultural and political forces urging it to shed its traditional responsibilities.[38]

Ambivalence and incoherence are reflected in the two different strands of community policing, which in many ways are at ideological odds with one another. The first model, zero tolerance, is based on neoconservative notions of a strong law-and-order presence. The second strand, what we characterized as a type of peace-corps framework, is a neoliberal approach that emphasizes citizen responsibility, prevention, and partnerships outside the criminal justice system. Although this ideological ambivalence is not always recognized by police academics and practitioners, the numerous debates that center on the desired future direction of community policing—Trojanowicz's vision versus Wilson's, for example—parallel the tensions in correctional reforms.

By placing the simultaneous police developments of democratization and militarization within a larger social control context, we can see that they are manifestations of a rapidly changing political and cultural landscape. Their coexistence demonstrates the inconsistencies and contradictions emanating from the state in late modernity. The discovery of a component of the police institution militarizing itself does not, therefore, illustrate the ascendance of state power.[39] To the contrary, it signals an attempt to maintain a small token of its dwindling prominence within the late modern society's complex of social controls.

Militarization and Democratization Working in Perfect Harmony?

As reasonable as the aforementioned sounds, there is more to this story. Empirical evidence derived from the real world of police practice complicates our explanation. In short, contemporary police practice may not be as incoherent and contradictory as an initial analysis might indicate.

The empirical evidence connecting paramilitary policing with community policing is overwhelming and is not an organizational secret. Kraska and Kappeler discovered that about two-thirds of the respondents to a national survey of small, medium, and large departments agreed that their police paramilitary units "play an important role in community policing strategies."[40] Remember that almost 20 percent of police departments use their PPUs for proactive patrol work. One participant in this practice made the interconnection clear.

> We conduct a lot of saturation patrol. We do terry stops and aggressive field interviews. These tactics are successful as long as the pressure stays on relentlessly. The key to our success is that we're an elite crime fighting team that's not bogged down in the regular bureaucracy. We focus on *quality of life* issues like illegal parking, loud music, bums, neighbor troubles. We have the freedom to stay in a hot area and clean it up—particularly gangs. Our tactical team works nicely with our department's emphasis on community policing.[41]

This quotation implies that there is no contradiction in having a paramilitary unit implement a central tenet of community policing—creating a climate of order. Another example of what we identified earlier as zero-tolerance community policing comes from an official of a highly acclaimed community policing department.

> We're into saturation patrols in hot spots. We do a lot of our work with the SWAT unit because we have bigger guns. We send out two, two-to-four-men cars, we look for minor violations and do jump-outs, either on people on the street or automobiles. After we jump-out the second car provides periphery cover with an ostentatious display of weaponry.[42]

Here we have an example of proactively targeting problematic space (hot spots) with roving squads of tactical officers, as opposed to the cop on the beat reacting to calls for service. The hot spot is usually identified using sophisticated geo-mapping computer analysis. This proactive orientation coincides with similar trends recognized by Feeley and Simon in the correctional field, where individualized punishments are being displaced by the "actuarial consideration of aggregates."[43] The next quotation, from a chief of police, mimics the ideology behind the governmental program known as "weed and seed" when discussing the role his PPU plays in community policing efforts.

> It's going to come to the point that the only people that are going to be able to deal with these problems [drugs, guns, gangs, and community disorder] are highly trained tactical teams with proper equipment to go into a neighborhood and clear the neighborhood and hold it; allowing community policing and problem oriented policing officers to come in and start turning the neighborhood around.[44]

Our final quotation illustrates an interesting application of the PPU no-knock dynamic entry approach:

ABC nightly news televised a 14-man PPU from Toledo, Ohio, based on a tip from the neighbor, conduct a no-knock dynamic entry on an average household (in other words, not a crackhouse). With MP5s slung, and in full paramilitary garb, the officers stormed the residence and aggressively threw people on the ground while ransacking the place for drugs. They found what they came for: less than an ounce of marijuana in one of the teenager's bedrooms. On the grounds of the Clinton Administration's Housing and Urban Development regulation termed, one strike and you're out, the police and media were excited to report that the entire family was evicted.[45]

This program illustrates how even the softer, regulatory aspects of community policing can be intertwined with the hard edge of paramilitary policing tactics. And as with the other quotations, in the realm of practice there is a type of harmony between community policing (at least the zero-tolerance strand) and paramilitary policing, as opposed to a tension or inconsistency. Apparently, some police agencies are integrating a military-model approach—occupy, suppress through force, and restore the affected territory—with community policing ideology, which emphasizes taking back the neighborhood, creating a climate of order, and enacting preventative and partnership strategies. Again, New York City's style of zero-tolerance community policing is the best-known example. Theoretically inspired by Wilson and Kelling's "broken windows" thesis, it seeks to maintain high police officer visibility, police-citizen information flows, incorporation of private and voluntary organizations, and the use of aggressive, militaristic tactics.[46]

Our analysis offers evidence, therefore, that the simultaneous rise of community and paramilitary policing should be seen at least partially as reflecting a consistent logic and coherence, not only volatility, contradiction, or incoherence. One of the foremost governmentality theorists points to our assessment as a real possibility. In arguing against the prevailing view of the criminal justice system as mired in incoherent rationalities and practices, Rose states that

despite their apparent complexity and heterogeneity, contemporary control strategies do show a certain strategic coherence. They can be broadly defined into two families: those that seek to regulate conduct by enmeshing individuals within circuits of inclusion and those that seek to act upon pathologies through managing a different set of circuits, circuits of exclusion.[47]

Rose goes on to conclude—after examining the consistency, logic, and ties that thread between the various circuits of control—that criminal justice control strategies do have a certain coherence. He rejects any notion that their coherence implies some sort of totalitarian control; his point is merely that seemingly contradictory rhetorics and practices do not necessarily operate in opposition to one another. The community policing/militarized policing paradox seems to be an important example.

Paradox, Strategic Coherence: What Does It Matter?

This chapter has attempted to make sense of the seeming contradiction in the simultaneous rise of police militarization and community policing. In doing so, we have attempted to review the literature about contemporary trends in corrections and policing, examine emerging theoretical frameworks for making sense of these trends, and provide a counterintuitive interpretation of the paradox based on observations of police practice.

We would like to conclude by exploring the implications of our analysis. Several are worth highlighting. First, the police studies literature, as opposed to focusing so heavily on which community policing reforms might work, needs to begin to document and make sense of the numerous controversial tactics emerging alongside community policing rhetoric. This neglect is helping to leave questionable police strategies, such as no-knock contraband raids and street sweeps, unchecked.

Second, strategies based on the military model and those based on a community policing model can be applied in an ideologically and operationally consistent manner. This may point to some serious shortcomings in the assumptions contained in community policing theory. Is it wise, for example, knowing the history of conservative police ideology and practice in the United States, to base a police reform agenda on the notion of creating a climate of order? Moreover, most would agree that the police have the ability to weed a location; what would make us think that they would have the will or ability to then seed it? At a minimum, our analysis should serve as a warning to well-intended community policing reformers to beware of unintended consequences.

Third, despite efforts by reformers to do away with the military-professional approach of the mid-1900s, the specter of the military model still haunts the real world of contemporary policing. Militarism is obviously an enduring and flexible presence that can adapt to changing external forces. As Haggerty and Ericson demonstrate in chapter 4, the military model can be influential in the realm of technological and information-based controls as well as the traditional use of force.

Fourth, the paradox-versus-strategic-coherence debate demonstrates that even if shifts in criminal justice policy may seem incompatible, one should not automatically assume that this signals confusion, incoherence, and volatility. Practitioners have the ability to maneuver through the tensions and pressures of external influences. It is not uncommon for them to have to amalgamate contradictory messages so that their real-world thinking and practice exhibit a level of coherence and harmony that makes sense to them. After all, has not the administration of justice always been fraught with contradictions through which practitioners have had to navigate? It does appear, however, that the rapid pace of change and intense volatility of late modern society will seriously test their abilities.

Finally, the governmentality framework teaches us that controls based on criminal justice are only a small part of the complex circuits of control characterizing contemporary society; the state's direct power to control citizens is diminishing. We hope that this chapter has demonstrated, though, that the police institution has a remarkable capacity to employ numerous strategies to resist the weakening of its authority. While police departments have embarked on an aggressive campaign to fight wars on drugs, gangs, and crime in poor inner-city communities, they are also interweaving themselves into the public school system as a permanent security, disciplinary, and educational presence. These varying roles of contemporary police might best be seen as reflecting coherence and stability, regardless of their apparently contradictory nature. Foucault's technologies of self and domination come together, often through conflict and rivalry, to form a significant part of the panoply of late modern control strategies.

Notes

1. See Malcolm Feeley and Jonathan Simon, "The New Penology: Notes on the Emerging Strategy of Corrections and Its Implications," *Criminology* 30 (1992): 449–74; "Actuarial Justice: The Emerging New Criminal Law," in *The Futures of Criminology,* ed. David Nelkin (Beverly Hills, Calif.: Sage, 1994); David Garland, *Punishment and Society* (Chicago: University of Chicago Press, 1990); "The Limits of the Sovereign State: Strategies of Crime Control in the Contemporary Society," *British Journal of Criminology* 36 (1996): 445–71; "The Culture of High Crime Societies: Some Preconditions of Recent Law and Order Policies," *British Journal of Criminology* 40 (2000): 347–75; Pat O'Malley, "Volatile and Contradictory Punishment," *Theoretical Criminology* 3 (1999): 175–96; John Pratt, "The Return of the Wheelbarrow Man, or The Arrival of the Postmodern Penality," *British Journal of Criminology* 40 (2000): 127–45; Nikolas Rose, "Government and Con-

trol," *British Journal of Criminology* 40 (2000): 321–39; Jonathan Simon, "They Died with Their Boots On: Boot Camps and the Limits of Modern Penality," *Social Justice* 22 (1995): 25–49.

2. Garland, "Culture of High Crime Societies," 348; "Limits of the Sovereign State."

3. Simon, "They Died with Their Boots On."

4. For more on civil asset forfeiture, see Henry Hyde, *Forfeiting Property Rights* (New York: Routledge, 1995), and Leonard Levy, *A License to Steal: The Forfeiture of Property* (Chapel Hill: University of North Carolina Press, 1996). For more on warrantless searches into public housing units, see C. Roush, "Warrantless Public Housing Searches: Individual Violations or Community Solutions," *American Criminal Law Review* 34 (1996): 261–88. For more on the use of surveillance equipment, see J. Fiske, "Surveilling the City: Whiteness, the Black Man, and Democratic Totalitarianism," *Theory, Culture, and Society* 15 (1998): 67–88, and Gary Marx, *Undercover: Police Surveillance in America* (Berkeley and Los Angeles: University of California Press, 1988). For more on police presence in American schools, see Peter Kraska and Matthew DeMichele, "Policing Our Nation's Schools: Issues and Trends," *Eastern Kentucky University Research Bulletin* (forthcoming). For more on police paramilitarism, see Peter Kraska and Victor Kappeler, "Militarizing American Police: The Rise and Normalization of Paramilitary Units," *Social Problems* 44 (1997): 1–18, and Peter Kraska and Louis Cubellis, "Militarizing Mayberry and Beyond: Making Sense of American Paramilitary Policing," *Justice Quarterly* 14 (1997): 607–29.

5. This point will be expanded in the conclusion; however, it should suffice to mention that we conceive of this reciprocal relation similarly to what Rose refers to as Foucault's "two, apparently illiberal, poles of power over life—the disciplines of the body and the biopolitics of the population"; see Nikolas Rose, "Governing Advanced Liberal Democracies," in *Foucault and Political Reason: Liberalism, Neo-Liberalism, and Rationalities of Government*, ed. Andrew Barry, Thomas Osborne, and Nikolas Rose (Chicago: University of Chicago Press, 1996), 44. What we intend to do here is demonstrate that these two discourses and technical strategies of control are inherently dependent upon one another in order to shape, guide, and program citizens' desires in accordance with political interests. In order to schematize this analysis, we conceptualize community policing rhetoric and practice, in accordance with Stenson, as technologies of the self, on the one hand, and envision police paramilitary units, on the other hand, as technologies of domination; see Kevin Stenson, "Community Policing as a Governmental Technology," *Economy and Society* 22 (1993): 373–89. However, we employ these conceptual devices not to demonstrate the distinction between these technologies of rule; rather, this paper explores, following Burchell, the "interconnections, continuities, and interactions between techniques of domination and techniques of the self"; see Graham Burchell, "Liberal Government and Techniques of the Self," in *Foucault and Political Reason: Liberalism, Neo-Liberalism, and Rationalities of Government*, ed. Andrew Barry, Thomas Osborne, and Nikolas Rose (Chicago: University of Chicago Press, 1996), 21.

6. This historical account of American policing is only meant to demonstrate the various administrative alterations in this modern institution. For a thorough account of the evolution of the contemporary police institution from the earlier notions of police science, see Franz-Ludwig Knemeyer, "Polizei," *Economy and Society* 9 (1980): 172–95; John McMullan, "Social Surveillance and the Rise of the Police Machine," *Theoretical Criminology* 2 (1998): 93–117; "The Arresting Eye: Discourse, Surveillance, and Disciplinary Administration in Early English Police Thinking," *Social and Legal Studies* 7 (1998): 97–128; Pasquale Pasquino, "Theatrum Politicum: The Genealogy of Capital-Police and the State of Prosperity," in *The Foucault Effect: Studies in Governmentality*, ed. Graham Burchell, Colin Gordon, and Peter Miller (Chicago: University of Chicago Press, 1991), 105–18.

7. On this issue, see Victor Kappeler, ed., *The Police and Society: Touchstone Readings*, 2d ed. (Prospect Heights, Ill.: Waveland, 1999), especially chapters 1–5.

8. Regardless of professional reforms, the police institution continued to exhibit extreme racial and gender mistreatment in both hiring practices and law enforcement functions, as

the riots of the 1960s in many American cities testify. For a "minority view" of police history, see Herbert Williams and Patrick Murphy, "The Evolving Strategy of Police: A Minority View," in *The Police and Society*, ed. Victor Kappeler (Prospect Heights, Ill.: Waveland, 1999), 27–50.

9. Chris Crowther, *Policing Urban Poverty* (London: Macmillan, 2000); Roger Hopkins Burke, "The Socio-Political Context of Zero Tolerance Policing Strategies," *Policing: An International Journal of Police Strategies and Management* 21 (1998): 666–82.

10. James Q. Wilson and George Kelling, "Broken Windows," in *The Police and Society*, ed. Victor Kappeler (Prospect Heights, Ill.: Waveland, 1999), 154–68; James Q. Wilson, *Thinking about Crime* (New York: Vintage, 1985), especially chapter 5.

11. Wilson and Kelling, "Broken Windows," 157.

12. Wilson and Kelling, "Broken Windows," 160.

13. See Pat O'Malley, "Policing, Politics, and Postmodernity," *Social and Legal Studies* 6 (1997): 363–81; Pat O'Malley and Darren Palmer, "Post-Keynesian Policing," *Economy and Society* 25 (1996): 137–55.

14. Robert Trojanowicz and Bonnie Bucqueroux, *Community Policing: How to Get Started*, 2d ed. (Cincinnati, Ohio: Anderson, 1998), 5.

15. See Pat O'Malley, "Risk, Power, and Crime Prevention," *Economy and Society* 21 (1992): 252–75; "Risk and Responsibility," in *Foucault and Political Reason: Liberalism, Neo-Liberalism, and Rationalities of Government*, ed. Andrew Barry, Thomas Osborne, and Nikolas Rose (Chicago: University of Chicago Press, 1996), 189–208; O'Malley and Palmer, "Post-Keynesian Policing"; Sean Watson, "Policing the Affective Society: Beyond Governmentality in the Theory of Social Control," *Social and Legal Studies* 8 (1999): 227–51.

16. See Garland, "The Limits of the Sovereign State"; O'Malley and Palmer, "Post-Keynesian Policing"; Stenson, "Community Policing."

17. See Kraska and Kappeler, "Militarizing American Police"; Kraska and Cubellis, "Militarizing Mayberry."

18. Kraska and Cubellis, "Militarizing Mayberry," 615.

19. Kraska and Cubellis, "Militarizing Mayberry," 619.

20. Kraska and Cubellis, "Militarizing Mayberry," 12.

21. Michel Foucault, "Governmentality," in *The Foucault Effect: Studies in Governmentality*, ed. Graham Burchell, Colin Gordon, and Peter Miller (Chicago: University of Chicago Press, 1991), 87–104.

22. Nikolas Rose, "Government, Authority, and Expertise in Advanced Liberalism," *Economy and Society* 22 (1993): 283–99; "Government and Control"; Nikolas Rose and Peter Miller, "Political Power beyond the State: Problematics of Government," *British Journal of Sociology* 43 (1992): 173–205.

23. On technologies of the self, see Graham Burchell, "Liberal Government and Techniques of the Self," *Economy and Society* 22 (1993): 267–82, reprinted in *Foucault and Political Reason: Liberalism, Neo-Liberalism, and Rationalities of Government*, ed. Andrew Barry, Thomas Osborne, and Nikolas Rose (Chicago: University of Chicago Press, 1996), 19–36.

24. See Rose, "Government, Authority, and Expertise"; Peter Miller and Nikolas Rose, "Governing Economic Life," *Economy and Society* 19 (1990): 1–31; Burchell, "Liberal Government and Techniques of the Self"; Graham Burchell, Colin Gordon, and Peter Miller, eds., *The Foucault Effect: Studies in Governmentality* (Chicago: University of Chicago Press, 1991).

25. Foucault, "Governmentality," 104.

26. Rose, "Government and Control," 323.

27. These heterogeneous agents and agencies, however, do not always function in a cooperative vacuum. Rather, these programs are often confronted by rivalries and competitions for scarce resources, which increase the likelihood of technologies appearing contradictive. Rose and Miller ("Political Power beyond the State," 190–91) summarize this possibility for competition: "Government is a congenitally failing operation. Technologies produce unexpected problems, are utilized for their own ends, [and] are hampered by under-funding, professional rivalries, and the impossibility of producing the technical conditions that

would make them work." These failures and rivalries encourage the discovery of something better and should be seen as contributing to the overall power of government, not in opposition of one another.

28. Stenson, "Community Policing."
29. O'Malley, "Volatile and Contradictory Punishment," 176.
30. Feeley and Simon, "The New Penology"; O'Malley, "Volatile and Contradictory Punishment"; Simon, "They Died with Their Boots On"; Garland, "The Limits of the Sovereign State," 445.
31. David Garland, "Penal Modernism and Postmodernism," in *Punishment and Social Control: Essays in Honor of Sheldon L. Messinger* (New York: Aldine De Gruyter, 1995), 201.
32. In this context, *welfare* refers to the "welfare states" that dominated much of the West at least until the end of World War II. This rationality of rule envisages a public dependent on the state to provide for its well-being "through state planning and intervention in the economy" and "the assembling of diverse mechanisms through which political forces link up a plethora of networks with aspirations to know, programme, and transform the social field" (Rose and Miller, "Political Power beyond the State," 191–92); see also Rose, "Governing Advanced Liberal Democracies"; "The Death of the Social"; Simon, "They Died with Their Boots On," n. 38.
33. Garland, "The Limits of the Sovereign State," 455–56.
34. See David Garland, *Punishment and Welfare* (Brookfield, Vt.: Gower, 1985), 93.
35. Garland, "The Limits of the Sovereign State," 446. On active citizenship, see O'Malley, "Risk, Power, and Crime Prevention"; "Risk and Responsibility."
36. Garland, "The Limits of the Sovereign State," 449.
37. Pratt, "The Return of the Wheelbarrow Man," 127; Simon, "They Died with Their Boots On."
38. Simon, "They Died with Their Boots On," 46, n. 43; Pratt, "The Return of the Wheelbarrow Man," 134.
39. Kraska and Kappeler, "Militarizing American Police," 13.
40. Kraska and Kappeler, "Militarizing American Police," 13.
41. Kraska and Cubellis, "Militarizing Mayberry," 624.
42. Kraska and Kappeler, "Militarizing American Police," 17.
43. Feeley and Simon, "The New Penology," 449.
44. Kraska and Cubellis, "Militarizing Mayberry," 625.
45. Kraska and Kappeler, "Militarizing American Police," 18.
46. See Crowther, *Policing Urban Poverty*; Hopkins Burke, "The Socio-Political Context"; R. R. Friedmann, *Community Policing: Comparative Perspectives and Prospects* (London: Harvester Wheatsheaf, 1992).
47. Rose, "Government and Control," 324.

Militarism Comes Home

Punishment, Feminism, and Popular Culture

———

Sacrificing Private Ryan

The Military Model and the New Penology

Jonathan Simon

Historians have long recognized the importance of the military as a model and a source of agents, ideas, and technologies for modern criminal justice institutions in the United States.[1] In the United States this influence remained relatively moderate. While it left permanent traits, such as the organization of police and prison agents into military-like ranks, the primary influences on rhetoric and practices of twentieth-century criminal justice came from elsewhere, including the labor market, medicine, the human sciences, and in the second half of the twentieth century, law. But now, at a time when modern penality seems to be undergoing profound changes, the military is reappearing as a source of content for criminal justice.[2] Examples abound. Police and more recently correctional staffs are being changed by the introduction of special weapons and tactical (SWAT) teams and other special groups that purport to be modeled on military special forces.[3] "Boot camps" purportedly modeled on military basic training installations have become one of the most popular variations on imprisonment over the last decades.[4] There are also signs of direct military linkage to criminal justice. One example is the involvement of military units in antidrug interdiction efforts. A second appeal has been raised for the military to open up at least some recruitment opportunities for graduates of correctional "boot camp."

This essay examines the increasing importance of the military as a model in criminal justice in the context of the host of social and cultural changes associated with postmodernity. At the end of their path-breaking analysis Kraska and Cubellis argue that paramilitary culture is being drawn into criminal justice institutions in response to the crisis of postmodernization that has undermined the traditional identities and practices associated with criminal justice.[5] They suggest that this represents both a falling back to premodern models of crime and war and a reaching forward toward post-modern models of criminal justice. This essay takes up the question of how paramilitary culture and practices address the needs of postmodern penality. I suggest that while military gestures may serve to make an increasingly large penal commitment more palatable to American political culture, they are dangerously misleading. Indeed, those aspects of American military culture that have supported rather than contradicted the values of American democracy are precisely those that are lacking in our emerging paramilitary penality. In his epic movie *Saving Private Ryan* (1999), Steven Spielberg focused on a central paradox of the military in twentieth-century American political culture: while the military has long been the very model of the sacrifice of individuality to the needs of faceless bureaucracy, it did so for the end of preserving an open and democratic society committed to the individual. This is perhaps why generations of Americans, especially those from discriminated-against minority groups, found in the military a boost toward equality. Ironically, the military is being touted as a model of penality at a moment when American penal policy has abandoned its historic commitment to both the individual and the idea of progressive transformation.

At the outset, it is useful to remind ourselves that the influences of the military on penality in both the past and the present has operated on multiple levels.

Rhetorics

Clearly the military has been an abundant source of symbolic material for the construction of criminal justice institutions, including uniforms, titles, and a host of specific practices and procedures.

Technologies and Rationalities of Power

The military was a major site for the development of modern bureaucratic forms so central to the rationalization of power in modernity.[6] In the nineteenth century, states looked to the military as a source of organizational technologies to build the new criminal justice institutions, especially police and prisons, that the rising demands for order in modern society seemed to require.[7] A crucial problem that these institutional planners needed to address was that of corruption, which Americans had long associated with European models of large government agencies. In fact, this process was always highly incomplete. Despite adoption of some military features in the nineteenth century, such as ranks and uniforms, the police as an organization never really imposed military discipline, remaining far more egalitarian and open to the influences (both good and bad) of the urban democratic society in which it operated.

Today we see a very different kind of technological borrowing. The police and prisons have adopted military tactics such as squads and teams with specialized tasks. While the nineteenth century transfers were aimed at making criminal justice institutions more acceptable to a public deeply skeptical of governmental power, current transfers are intended to intensify the instrumental capacity of criminal justice institutions to address criminal threats perceived as more invidious and distinct than in the past.

Mentalities

A third kind of institutional transfer concerns mentalities understood as complexes of emotional and cognitive attributes that form more or less durable structures sustained in large part by rituals, narratives, and incentives of various sorts. It is mentalities we have in mind when we talk about boot camps turning disorderly civilians into fighting machines, or first-year law school classes teaching students how to "think like a lawyer." The military has long been a productive source of mentalities (along with the technologies of power to produce them). For example, concepts such as loyalty, duty, and obedience to rank describe mental attributes that the military does not presume; rather, recruits must internalize them and officers must excel in them. All three concepts have been widely borrowed by other institutions seeking to establish discipline and motivate performance. While we often treat aggression as a natural or instinctual property of human beings, the military has long recognized that the capacity to use violence against others is one that must be trained for. As Paul Chevigny points out, these different strands of influence are combined in complex ways by contemporary police agencies.[8] In their analysis of contemporary policing in the United States, Kraska and Cubellis likewise suggest that multiple logics of influence might be unfolding.[9]

These arguments suggest that one should be wary of the implication that the increasingly paramilitary features of criminal justice agencies represent a coherent and comprehensive top-down strategy. Rather, what we see happening in policing and corrections today may be a product of multiple, overlapping, and heterodox borrowings from the military of different kinds of influences by different sectors and interests within the receiving institutions. The result is more pastiche than program.

What Are the Problems to Which the Military Model Looks Like a Solution?

As both David Rothman and Michel Foucault taught us, the history of penality is a history of failure and regrets. But since the late 1960s there are signs that penal institutions in the United States and many other industrial democracies have been undergoing greater than normal strain.[10] Here I will touch on only those aspects of this crisis relevant to the importation of rhetorics, rationalities, and mentalities from the military into criminal justice. Perhaps the single most important strain facing criminal justice institutions in the United States today has been the dramatic collapse of long-standing internal narratives and robust organizational cultures since the early 1970s. By narratives I mean the set of stories through which any occupational group articulates its values and virtues. The importance of narrative goes beyond the role of legitimation. Narratives provide a way for criminal justice agents to describe their role to their targets, to their public audience, and just as importantly to themselves, in a way that may bolster the appearance and sense of competence and propriety. They also help shape the practical forms of social organization that are developed within criminal justice institutions.[11] For most of the twentieth century, the dominant narratives of criminal justice emphasized professionalism, scientific authority, and benevolent goals of treatment and rehabilitation. These narratives, which can be described as "modernist," underwent a stunningly rapid collapse in the 1970s, captured in the immensely influential if misleading notion that with respect to crime, "nothing works." After more than a century in which it seemed that criminal justice agencies, no matter their problems, would improve as they became more professional, more scientific, and more treatment oriented, all of these values became problematic within less than a decade. The immense growth of criminal justice institutions in the United States during the 1980s and 1990s, especially corrections, exacerbated the collapse of the dominant narratives by tremendously diluting the organizational cultures built up over decades, washing away those elements of the modernist narratives that survived in local institutions. As the need for new correctional officers and somewhat later police officers boomed with the rising tide of "get tough" penal legislation (itself a reflection of the collapse of the modernist narratives), agencies found themselves hiring many new recruits. The discrediting of the older narratives and the flood of new recruits undermined the traditional spread of organizational culture from one generation of workers to the next.

There is, to be sure, a strong narrative about crime available in the culture. Since the 1970s a populist punitiveness has arisen to become a central aspect of political discourse.[12] Politicians of various political ideologies and at all levels and branches of government have responded. But while these narratives of punishment have clearly helped support the rapid growth of the correctional population and the size of the penal system, they provide little if any real support to the organizational needs of criminal justice institutions and their agents for explanation and interpretation. The rhetoric of "getting tough" and "accountability" for criminals may encourage sending more offenders to prison for longer sentences but helps little in determining how to deal with offenders once they are in prison. Likewise, police officers may hear these popular slogans as encouragement, but they provide little in practical guidance (especially when "getting tough" with arrestees may result in lawsuits and dismissals of charges). While populist punitiveness has helped make the clinical discourse associated with rehabilitation unacceptable, it has not produced alternatives. It is noteworthy in this respect that despite the discrediting of rehabilitation we still call prisons "correctional facilities" and prison staff "correctional officers." Despite over two decades of "getting tough," there are no prisons described as "vengeance centers" or "punishment institutions."

The collapse of the penal narratives associated with normalization on the inside has corresponded to, and been caused in part by, transformations on the outside that have made the task of suppressing crime (the job of both police and the penal system) more intractable. The rise of both modern police and modern penal institutions paralleled the growth of an urban working class in the United States. The most disadvantaged segments of the working classes have long been the primary subjects of police and penal work. The hardening of that disadvantaged sector, largely composed of racial and ethnic minorities, and its separation from the labor market into a kind of "underclass" have made traditional informal strategies of control less effective. Likewise, institutions such as factories, the merchant marines, and the military, which once absorbed young men in danger of falling into criminal careers, have retrenched in the face of deindustrialization and other social and economic changes associated with postmodernization. In combination these changes in the narrative and strategic context of penal work have forced penal institutions to look for new sources of both. In the remaining sections of this essay I want to follow two distinct pathways that seem to be bringing military models back into penality: paramilitary culture and the cyborg phenomenon.

Paramilitary Culture, "New War," and Penal Narratives since the 1960s

According to James Gibson, the Vietnam War defined a new model of war for American popular culture that he calls "New War."[13] In movies and novels the images formed by World Wars I and II were replaced by a whole set of Vietnam-based scenarios. In the old war model, distinct national forces fought discrete battles for position across a territory with contested boundaries and for populations with relatively consistent solidarities. In the new war model exemplified by the Vietnam War, small units of often ambiguous national identity fight a comparatively low-level but almost continuous war, largely devoid of fixed positions on territory, and in the midst of populations whose solidarities remain fundamentally untrustworthy. New War transforms not only the strategies of war but also the narratives that wars generate through popular culture. New Wars allow for temporary victories and defeats, but they are largely beyond any clear sense of liberation or occupation.

Gibson argues that the trauma of America's involvement in the Vietnam War, combined with a whole series of internal "culture" wars that were fought inside the United States over much the same period around the maintenance of traditional privileges based on race, gender, and sexual orientation, dramatically eroded the confidence of many Americans in our reigning national institutions and narratives. For many people, especially white males who felt the most threatened by the prospect of cultural change, New War emerged as a more general model of the whole range of threats facing America, including crime and drugs, welfare dependency, and illegal immigration.

Gibson's analysis provides a useful opening to examine how changing

popular narratives of crime and punishment relate to the narratives produced by the criminal justice system and its various adjuncts. The Vietnam
War took place contemporaneously with a rise in violent crime to levels not
seen for decades previously in most American cities. This was particularly
ominous given the fact that wars usually suppress crime by incapacitating
otherwise crime-prone young males in the service of their country. The sense
that American cities were being transformed into dangerous and unfamiliar
landscapes was exacerbated by the series of civil disturbances in African
American inner-city neighborhoods and the sometimes violent antiwar protests that broke out in otherwise pastoral campus settings such as Ann
Arbor, Michigan, and Madison, Wisconsin.

American attitudes and practices related to crime are an important component of this broad change. Two broad areas of change on this issue stand
out. First, a long-term trend in American public opinion toward support
for less punitive and stigmatizing ways of treating criminal offenders was
reversed. Support for the death penalty and for more severe prison sentences
was growing by the early 1970s and came to reach overwhelming majority
support during the next two decades.[14] Second, fear of crime has come to be
a pervasive influence on all aspects of middle-class life. Many people with
the means to do so, especially those with children, have sought to physically
dislocate themselves from perceived urban danger zones. Even in the safer
suburbs, however, life reflects a comprehensive concern with preventing
crime, including extensive investment in private security forces, alarm systems, and for those who can afford to move there, fully gated communities
from which all strangers (sometimes even postal workers and newspaper
carriers) are excluded. This trend is particularly evident in the rise of perva-
sively managed lifestyles for children, who are perceived as most vulnerable
to the crime threat. The era when children were sent outside to play has
been replaced by rigorously managed schedules of taking children to and
from one supervised activity after another. Both trends have fed the boom-
ing penal population and the growing size of police forces across the country. Although physical displacement and imprisonment might be taken as
alternative ways for a middle class to seek protection against what it per-
ceives as an out-of-control criminal class, the two have actually fed upon
each other. The increasingly managed space of the suburbs creates greater
levels of anxiety by contrast with the media-fed images of urban chaos,
while the burgeoning prison population feeds the perception that crime is
out of control.

The complex of cultural associations that Gibson describes as New War is reflected in the obsession with crime that is fueling both of these trends. New War culture emphasizes the wholly evil and pernicious nature of those who threaten our security. In this model neither war nor crime reflects genuine conflicts of interest among groups or classes of people. Instead, both are perceived as the products of evil individuals motivated by ultimately demonic forces. In war this precludes any real hope of negotiated solution and presages the need for utter ruthlessness by the forces of good if they are to have a chance against unrelenting evil. In crime this means the abandonment of any requirement that government seek to rehabilitate or reintegrate offenders. Punishment, as severe as possible, is warranted by the need to incapacitate enemies that can be neither transformed into friends nor even deterred from aggression, but only contained or eliminated. Criminal offenders are seen as both motivated and efficient predators whose taking pleasure in crime justifies a reciprocal satisfaction with the knowledge of the offender's grim fate. Gibson argues that popular culture increasingly gives vent to these vengeful pleasures, for example, in the *Rambo* movies. But precisely the same invitation to sadism in the name of good may be found in crime films such as the *Dirty Harry* movies or even a film that allegedly takes a liberal view of punishment such as *The Green Mile*.

A second New War element in crime thinking is the destabilizing of the idea of a common territory to be liberated or made secure by the action of government. Like foreign New War enemies, contemporary urban crime is viewed as embedded in social contexts that are themselves a source of contamination and danger. Since the 1960s police have been seen less as maintaining a thin blue line around a common settlement, and more as lone patrols going into territories that can never really be liberated from crime. Even the more recent formation of gated communities suggests the model of permanently militarized strategic hamlets that American military planners touted as a partial solution to the intractable nature of enemy penetration in South Vietnam. Since even the most vigorous law enforcement and severe punishments can only make the threat of crime manageable but never eliminate it, policing, punishment, and high-security homesteads are justified as permanent aspects of life.

These New War themes are also found in the growth of new penal practices and discourses. One of the most significant concerns the recently popular "Supermax" prisons that states and the federal government have built in recent years to hold their allegedly most violent offenders. These new prisons combine military-like organization of special teams with high-technology environments designed to minimize any element of communication and exchange among inmates or between inmates and staff. The result is a relationship more akin to war than to the factories on which nineteenth-century penitentiary prisons were based. In a sense, the old prison-as-factory model was a version of normal industrial life with its coercive aspects heightened but not beyond all recognition. In contrast, Supermax prisons, like other aspects of New War culture, imagine that crime can never be normalized but only endlessly fought.

Although the Supermax seems to be becoming a more general model for prisons, the design was originally justified by the need to respond to prison gangs, which have been viewed as the dominant threat to prison order since the 1970s. Whatever their real nature (something almost impossible to determine now that sociologists have largely been banned from our prisons), the way prison gangs are represented to the public closely resembles the "terrorist" enemies popularly represented in New War fiction. Likewise, the permanently installed paramilitary teams in the Supermax institution closely parallel the vision of the good guys in New War fiction: not the regular army, but tightly knit teams designed to operate with superefficiency and the ruthlessness to match their adversaries. Indeed, further research (were it possible) might show that it is New War popular culture that is setting the agenda for our prison policies.

Traditional modern narratives provided a flexible and productive ideology for criminal justice agents to organize and make sense of the power to punish as part of a general effort to provide discipline, sociability, and opportunities for a population of those marginal to the labor market but not exiled from it. In this regard prisons and their agents were part of a broader practice of governing through the dynamic of social life itself, including the family, the labor market, and the community. Schools, public health, social insurance and welfare, police, and penal institutions could be rationalized through the master problem of "society," and the complex web of scientific and reform discourses provided expertise on social problems through the first three-quarters of the twentieth century. But in the last thirty years the "social" has been increasingly discredited as a platform for governing.[15] We see this in the declining prestige of those institutions and strategies that invoked the very nature of the social, including social welfare, social work, social security, and social insurance. We can also observe this in the relative decline in the prestige of sociology as an academic and governmental discourse since the 1970s. Paramilitary culture and Gibson's New War reflect the discrediting of the social and its related narratives.

The old military symbolized by the draft was a powerful simile for society as a material object. The great military inductions for World Wars I and II generated enormous opportunities to produce statistical knowledge about the male population and its health, intelligence, and behavior. Not surprisingly, military sociology has been a central field within the discipline since that time. But by the 1970s, notwithstanding traditional forms of popular culture celebration (such as John Wayne's *Green Berets*), the Vietnam-era military (again a conscripted army) became symbolic of the bloated and incompetent bureaucracies that conservative politicians generally painted liberal government as producing. Indeed, the public threats to order in the Vietnam-era military—rampant drug use, widespread flouting of discipline, and incidents of lethal violence against officers—were parallel to those seemingly afflicting American society in general. The military model reconfigured in real and imaginary terms after Vietnam now offers a more attractive alternative. The model of the military special forces unit contrasts well with the older military model of immersion in a mass force. As reflected in dozens of "boot camp" movies produced for World War II, the army was about unity and homogeneity within the great mass. The power of a movie like Steven Spielberg's *Saving Private Ryan* lies precisely in playing this mass off against the individualism to which democratic society was dedicated. The special forces unit, in contrast, offers a model of a small community and an opportunity for satisfying personal needs as well as organizational objectives.

In this section I have tried to argue that contemporary criminal justice is adopting paramilitary features in response to the discrediting of the same modernist narratives, with their emphasis on society and commitment to democratic individualism, that shaped perceptions of the military prior to the Vietnam War. In its New War guise, the military offers a whole complex of associations that address the gap opened up by the loss of those narratives. With its Manichean landscape of total evil and transcendent good, paramilitary culture and populist punitiveness replace the old dialectic of mass and individual with a new picture of small groups surviving through a capacity to match the violence and ruthlessness of their enemies. If there is one piece of contemporary culture that best symbolizes both the military and criminal justice side of this new logic it is the enormously popular "sport utility vehicle" (SUV), with its direct invocation of military equipment and its implicit assumption that common social assets such as adequate roads and safe public spaces have become extinct. The fact that SUVs have become the most popular motor vehicles in America suggests how deeply even the most affluent and secure Americans now feel that they are surrounded by hostile and desperate enemies and how little faith they have in any collective solutions to our social problems (problems generally exacerbated by these vehicles).

Cyborgs and Systems

Paramilitary culture provides one motivation for criminal justice institutions to remake themselves in the popular image of the military. Much of this fits with what I identified as "rhetorics" in the introduction. A second motivation lies in the increasing importance of new rationalities and technologies of power associated with the rise of high-technology machines and forms of thinking, especially the growing role of "cyborgs" to the exercise of power in postmodern society. According to the political theorist Donna Haraway, "the cyborg is a cybernetic organism, a fusion of the organic and the technical forged in particular, historical, cultural practices."[16] The astronaut in a space suit is one of the earliest and most widely dispersed images of a cyborg. Other examples of cyborgism in contemporary culture include computer chips, genes, databases, smart bombs, the ultrasound-represented fetus, and even the "ecosystem." In popular culture they have become even more common. Figures such as the Terminator, RoboCop, and Data have become celebrities.[17] Taking a cue from the popularity of these fictional cyborgs, Haraway argues persuasively that we need to reject the reactive tendency to see the cyborg as a wholly negative threat to some kind of essential humanity. Instead, cyborgs are a site of emergence for new possibilities of being human with both disturbing and exciting implications.

The rise of cyborgs and the systems thinking that goes with them has been a response to the pervasive legitimation crisis of authority that has been a noted feature of the advanced postindustrial societies since the 1960s. As faith in democratic decision making has declined, the quest for mechanical systems to remove judgment from political debate has grown. One example is the enormous popularity of constitutional amendments that take decisions about taxation and financing out of the hands of elected legislatures. Criminal justice institutions have been among those parts of democratic societies most undermined by the legitimation crisis. Parole boards, judges, and even police officers are seen as too unreliable in exercising discretion. In their place states and the federal government have adopted determinate sentencing systems, mandatory terms, and laws requiring arrest (for example, in domestic violence cases).

The post–World War II military is one key sector from which the techno-science discourses that sustain cyborgs have taken shape. Weapon systems combining technical and human components in semiautonomous units have been an important part of twentieth-century war. From out of the experience with technologically advanced weapons such as tanks and airplanes came the beginnings of operations research and later systems analysis and cybernetics. Operations research was originally just the collection of statistics on the performance of specific weapons. Systems analysis built from this kind of data far more ambitious weapons and strategies. Cybernetics, a term that has gone out of fashion, referenced a broad vision of an interdisciplinary science of human affairs based on the analysis of systems of all types—human, natural, and machine. These scientific discourses became central first to the organization of atomic weapons in the 1940s and 1950s. They became a dominant discourse of governance within the military itself during the 1960s, when Secretary of Defense Robert McNamara introduced systems analysis into all the services and the conduct of the war in Vietnam. The contemporary military continues to be dominated by systems thinking, with its heavy reliance on quantifiable data and computers.

The flow of military cyborgs and systems thinking into penality is extensive, and documenting its path would constitute an extended research project of its own. A highly visible example, though, is the Rand Corporation, a private not-for-profit organization that has produced military and social policy expertise for half a century. Rand, whose name is a condensation of the phrase "research and development," grew from a small operation within the MacDonald Douglas Aircraft Company in the 1940s, to the air force, and later to independence in 1948. One of Rand's primary extensions beyond defense policy has been criminal justice. Rand scientists have published some of the most influential criminological research of the last two decades, including studies of racial discrimination in sentencing and selective incapacitation.

The cyborg and systems analysis features moving into criminal justice institutions are often coextensive with New War features, and both have been influential in transforming contemporary penality. Again, the increasingly popular Supermax prison provides an example. The correctional special response teams, equipped with high-technology chemical and electrical weapons and coordinated by tightly scripted battle plans, are cyborgs. So are the cells and indeed the entire structure of the new Supermax prisons, in which both prisoners and correctional officers are embedded in a system of high-tech controls. The inmates of Supermax prisons are also cyborgs, embedded in machine systems that mediate their every interaction. The classic penitentiary made the individual offender the target of penal exercises of power. Despite its superficial resemblance, the Supermax is based on something quite different. Now the cell/inmate cyborg, thickened with layers of machine technology, is the real target of power, power that cannot fail because it is hard-wired into its subject. In a broader sense, the Supermax prison as a whole is a kind of cyborg in which human elements are mutually locked into a machine system.

The Supermax also embodies features of systems analysis. Perhaps the central value that systems analysis teaches is recycling performance information into ongoing tactical adjustments and into long-term strategic planning. Of course, all ways of governing attempt this to some extent. Systems analysis takes this to a higher level by forging durable information flows out of mechanisms and opportunities for counting things and channels for collecting and distributing the data. The paradox of this approach is that to be flexible and effective at the system level, you must have rigid controls on the micro level of data creation. The Supermax prison is designed to quantify and accumulate information about itself continuously. The special response teams exemplify the broader pattern in these prisons of control through programs of tightly enforced rules. For example, the cell extraction procedures described above are regulated by rule systems that determine specific levels of inmate disobedience that trigger an extraction. At one prison, once an extraction has been officially triggered, the team must go forward with their function regardless of whether the inmate decides to submit peacefully once confronted by the team. Ironically, the systemic rationality of these prisons and tactics may make them easier for courts to police for constitutional violations.

Conclusion

This essay suggests that the increasingly visible pattern of military influences on criminal justice is a result of overlapping motivations operating at different levels of criminal justice institutions. One motive is the need for criminal justice personnel at all levels to find suitable narratives through which to explain their roles and interpret the world they encounter. We see this in penal institutions in the creation of special units that parallel the military special forces and the embrace of a "war on crime" mentality by staff across the board in many of these institutions. Much of the content of this narrative comes not from actual experience in the military but from the dispersed elements of popular culture that James Gibson calls New War. Intertwined within this paramilitary culture is a drive to further rationalize an increasingly large and expensive sector of public spending through the transfer of cyborgs and operating protocols based on systems analysis.

It is premature to ask whether these adaptations will succeed in forging a new penal model as successful as the industrial and clinical ones that sustained modern penal institutions for most of the last century. What made the industrial factory and the medical clinic such effective schemas for penality is that they addressed three audiences with different needs: (1) the agents of punishment, who almost always are in need of effective explanations of what they are doing and how; (2) the managers, who need governance systems that can be used to effectively control both their inmates and staffs; and (3) the public, which needs models of punishment that can provide a sense of security and progress. For reasons suggested above, the first two needs are being effectively met by paramilitary culture and the new models of management and organization that are coming out of the military. At the same time, there are real questions as to whether these new narratives and strategies can address the needs of the public. Indeed, the very thing that seems to motivate paramilitary culture and the technologies of power associated with cyborgs is a kind of permanent public insecurity.

Notes

This chapter is a revised version of "Paramilitary Features of Contemporary Penality," *Journal of Political and Military Sociology* 27, no. 2 (1999): 279–90.

1. See David J. Rothman, *The Discovery of the Asylum: Social Order and Disorder in the New Republic* (Toronto: Little Brown, 1971); Michel Foucault, *Discipline and Punish: The Birth of the Prison*, trans. Alan Sheridan (New York: Pantheon, 1977).
2. See Stanley Cohen, *Visions of Social Control: Crime, Punishment, and Classification* (Cambridge: Polity, 1985); David Garland, *Punishment and Modern Society* (Chicago: University of Chicago Press, 1990); Malcolm Feeley and Jonathan Simon, "The New Penology: Notes on the Emerging Strategy of Corrections and Its Implications," *Criminology* 30 (1992): 449–74.
3. See Peter B. Kraska and Louis J. Cubellis, "Militarizing Mayberry and Beyond: Making Sense of American Paramilitary Policing," *Justice Quarterly* 14 (1997): 607–29.
4. See Jonathan Simon, "They Died with Their Boots On: The Boot Camp and the Limits of Modern Penality," *Social Justice* 22 (1995): 25–48.
5. Kraska and Cubellis, "Militarizing Mayberry," 625.
6. See Max Weber, *Economy and Society*, ed. Guenther Roth and Claus Wichita (Berkeley and Los Angeles: University of California Press, 1968), 221–23.
7. See Paul Chevigny, *Edge of the Knife: Police Violence in the Americas* (New York: New Press, 1994).

8. Chevigny, *Edge of the Knife,* 255–56.
9. Kraska and Cubellis, "Militarizing Mayberry," 625–26.
10. See Garland, *Punishment and Modern Society*; Jonathan Simon, *Poor Discipline: Parole and the Social Control of the Urban Underclass, 1890–1990* (Chicago: University of Chicago Press, 1993).
11. See Charles Bright, *The Powers That Punish: Prison and Politics in the Era of the "Big House," 1920–1955* (Ann Arbor: University of Michigan Press, 1995).
12. See Diana Gordon, *The Justice Juggernaut: Fighting Street Crime, Controlling Citizens* (New Brunswick, N.J.: Rutgers University Press, 1991); Stuart Scheingold, *The Politics of Street Crime: Criminal Process and Cultural Obsession* (Philadelphia: Temple University Press, 1991); Jonathan Simon and Malcolm Feeley, "True Crime: The New Penology and Public Discourse on Crime," in *Punishment and Social Control: Essays in Honor of Sheldon Messinger,* ed. Thomas G. Blomberg and Stanley Cohen (New York: Aldine DeGruyter, 1995), 147–80.
13. James Gibson, *Warrior Dreams: Paramilitary Culture in Post-Vietnam America* (New York: Hill and Wang, 1994).
14. See Phoebe Ellsworth and Samuel Gross, "Hardening of the Attitudes: Americans' Views on the Death Penalty," *Journal of Social Issues* 50 (1994): 19–52.
15. See Jean Baudrillard, *In the Shadow of the Silent Majorities, or The Death of the Social* (New York: Semiotexte, 1983); Nikolas Rose, "The Death of the Social? Re-figuring the Territory of Government," *Economy and Society* 25 (1996): 327–56.
16. See Donna Haraway, *ModestWitness@SecondMillennium: FemaleMan™ Meets OncoMouse™: Feminism and Technoscience* (New York: Routledge, 1997), 51.
17. As these examples show, the image of the cyborg as a fusion between a singular human and some set of machines embodied in the spacesuited astronaut is too narrow. Wholly organic entities may be considered cyborgism when they operate in a space wholly defined by machines, whether the fetus on the ultrasound or the brain captured in the measurements of new imaging devices. Likewise, complex entities such as the ecosystem may include biological entities and largely conceptual technologies.

Militarism, Feminism, and Criminal Justice

Challenging Institutionalized Ideologies

Susan L. Caulfield

If you insist upon fighting to protect me, or our country, let it be understood, soberly and rationally between us, that you are fighting to protect benefits which I have not shared and probably will not share; but not to gratify my instincts, or to protect either myself or my country. In fact, as a woman, I have no country. As a woman, I want no country. As a woman, my country is the whole world.

Virginia Woolf, Three Guineas

I approached the writing of this piece as an antimilitarist, feminist, and peace activist. I have sat with the subject of militarism and war for many years, always knowing there were ties to my studying and teaching of criminal justice. What I present here is a continuing conversation on militarism, informed by voices from feminist perspectives.

I have always struggled for peace and social justice. I was, as the phrase goes, a "military brat." I was raised in a military family, held most of my early jobs on military bases, and spent my youth at parades that featured marching soldiers, tanks, and various armaments of artillery. For many of these years, I questioned existing arrangements and struggled to define myself as a woman and as a person. As a woman having lived the first twenty-five years of my life within military settings, I have experienced both patriarchy and militarism firsthand. Such experiences are important to the arguments made herein, as immersion in a military environment drives home the privileging of nationalism, patriotism, and the supremacy of the state.

That I have built a career in criminal justice is no accident. As Richard Quinney points out, it is important to bear witness to harmful arrangements so that change can come about.[1] What follows, then, is my witnessing of militarism and feminism and the implications for criminal justice.

This chapter examines the intersecting points of militarism, feminism, and the study of crime and criminal justice. Militarism is an important concept that heretofore has been given little attention in the criminal justice literature. Examining the role of militarism is a logical extension of work in both feminist and peacemaking criminology, because it is a tool to explore further the impact of patriarchy, masculinity, racism, sexism, and dominant ideology. Instead of looking at existing criminal justice policy as natural, innate, expected, or effective, it helps to take an approach that questions the roots of such policy.

As feminists who have written about class and race as well as sex will attest, the arrangements that foster inequality and violence are not only about men. A newer addition to the complexity of this mix is, I believe, militarism. An antimilitarist feminist approach examines these roots and describes the consequences of policy developed from such a heritage. Importantly, the antimilitarist feminist approach taken herein is one that focuses on social arrangements, such as violence, as central factors for evaluating social policy, especially criminal justice policy. As David Gil instructs, if we do not address the social sources of violence, any attempts to eliminate violence will be fruitless.[2] I suggest here that militarism is a key source of violence in U.S. society and for that reason must be examined.

In further developing the conversation on militarism, feminism, and criminal justice, what becomes apparent is the role of social arrangements in the perpetuation of harmful practices. The exploration of social arrangements is informed by an understanding of militarism, then contrasted with arrangements proposed by feminists. The consequences of both are examined regarding criminal justice policy.

Examining the impact of militarism through a feminist lens seems a logical step in the development of feminist theory. Early feminist approaches helped us to understand social arrangements when they emphasized the gendered (patriarchal) dimension of society. Socialist feminists added class (capitalism) to the analysis, while feminists of color added race and ethnicity to the equation. As the next step, antimilitarist feminists can demonstrate the overall privileging of power, control, and violence, which harms all groups, by looking at militarist ideology. Militarism best describes the us-versus-them mentality that is likely at the root of most "-ism" schisms in U.S. society. In a culture born out of revolution, called upon to defend freedom, and newly sprung from the Cold War, militarist values are deeply ingrained.

It is not my intent to frame the contrast between militarism and feminism as a male-versus-female conflict. To analyze feminism and masculinism from a structural perspective should not be construed as equating the characteristics of each as essentially the characteristics of individuals. bell hooks sums up this point nicely by drawing our attention to how both men and women have played key roles in the perpetuation of militarism, as they have in the perpetuation of today's criminal justice system.[3] In short, not all men glorify war, and not all women are peacemakers. Instead, by using the framework of feminism and militarism, we may seek a broader understanding of both criminology and criminal justice and find ways to move ourselves and our institutions toward the peaceful resolution of conflict.

Scholars of criminology and criminal justice, by taking an increasingly more accepting stance toward feminist perspectives, have learned that feminism helps fill in many of the gaps in what was previously known about the nature of crime and the operations of criminal justice. What is still unknown to most of these scholars is how a study of militarism can likewise help increase our understanding of crime and criminal justice. While there is sound research on militarism and its effects, this research is not found in overviews of crime and criminal justice. In fact, one would be hard pressed to find any mention of militarism within discussions of social factors that impact crime and criminal justice. Even within the area of peacemaking criminology, there is little to be found on militarism; what comes closest are references to war (e.g., the war on drugs, the war on poverty, and the war on crime). Pepinsky and Quinney's text *Criminology as Peacemaking* captures much of what has been done in the area of peacemaking criminology, yet it offers little discussion on the role of militarism within U.S. society in general and criminal justice in particular.[4]

What follows is a brief introduction to the role of militarism in U.S. society, with an emphasis on the importance of understanding the concomitant social arrangements and resulting ideology. Much of this introduction is informed by feminist scholars of militarism, as their work often focuses on values and beliefs. This is followed by a discussion of how feminism has expanded the scope of criminology and, in doing so, has helped push the boundaries of traditional criminology. Also there is an overview of beliefs and values often touted as feminist, with discussion of how adherence to such values would alter the social arrangements of U.S. society. Lastly, there is a discussion of the implications of militarist and feminist approaches to policy, with the intent to show how criminology and criminal justice might benefit from such an examination.

The Role of Militarism

Before examining the role of militarism in U.S. society or the criminal justice system, it is important to establish what is meant by *militarism*. In his book *Organizing Societies for War*, Patrick Regan presents three definitions that are an important foundation for the discussion herein:

1. *Militarized*: a condition reflecting the extent to which civil society is organized around the preparation for war
2. *Militarization*: the process by which states move from a less militarized condition toward a more militarized one
3. *Militarism*: refers to military-based values and ideals[5]

Regan further elaborates on militarism by quoting Crawford:

> Militarism is a coherent set of beliefs about the nature of the international system and the best ways to get along in it. Militarists assume that the use of force in international relations is natural, expected, and effective in most instances and they recognize few limits to the effective use of force.[6]

In addition, citing Gillis, Regan notes that "militarism is . . . the prevalence of warlike values in a society."[7] Feinman's definition of militarism is instructive: "Militarism is an ideology . . . an acceptance of organized state violence as a legitimate solution to conflict." In addition, "militarism is defined as . . . the deep conditioning of the society to valorize military cultures."[8] Therefore, to understand the role of militarism, it is necessary to examine the values and beliefs of U.S. society. As Carlton notes, "Values are enshrined in ideologies, and values are really preference statements. This means that their relative merits cannot be scientifically validated. But in institutional terms, they can be 'realized,' promoted, and even enforced. . . . ideologies are forms of belief-system that explain and justify a preferred social order."[9]

In U.S. society, a dominant ideology—an often unquestioned set of beliefs—informs the development of institutions, while, in a circular relationship, the same institutions, through their functioning, lend support to the dominant ideology. For example, the support for the cultural norm of "rugged individualism" in U.S. society comes not only from historical folklore, such as taming the Wild West and settling the colonies. Support also comes from educational institutions that promote the work of the individual as opposed to the group. This belief is also lent support by policies that suggest that families ought to be able to survive on their own, without the need for governmental subsidies. Rugged individualism is further supported by economics (i.e., pull yourself up by your bootstraps and you, too, can be successful), and by the institution of social control. As for the latter, criminal law is written such that individuals are held accountable for illegal behavior (with the consequence that corporations are often not held accountable). All persons are influenced by the prevailing ideology as it affects how each person is socialized. Then, through support of existing institutional practices, the ideology is given additional strength and life. All of the dominant institutions lend support to ideology, as do all dominant practices.

From a budgetary viewpoint alone, the military clearly must be considered one of the dominant institutions of U.S. society. As Felice notes, "Over 42 percent of the entire world's military expenditures are made by the United States. The federal government spends four times as much on the military as on education, job training, housing, economic development, and environmental protection combined."[10] The military far surpasses in spending the other major institutions of U.S. society.

For the public to be persuaded of the importance of militarism, the values of militarism must be rooted in the political and social life of the state. These values include hierarchy, discipline, obedience, and centralization of authority.[11] In the United States, numerous hierarchies are based on traits such as sex, race, social class, and political affiliation. Within patriarchy, masculine and not feminine characteristics are rewarded. Along with gender hierarchy comes socialization into gender roles, which leads to beliefs that males should dominate in relationships while females should be subservient and obey. Belief in the legitimacy of these arrangements results in harmful behavior. Behavior such as the battering of women is created out of structural arrangements such as these. Research has demonstrated that a strong commitment to hierarchy, domination, and control allows batterers to believe that what they are doing is acceptable.[12]

Importantly, as Klein notes, "men are structurally and psychologically accustomed to taking it out on women."[13] Such practices have become commonplace and tolerated in U.S. society. Tolerance results from ideologies, "ideologies which assume that most rapes are really seduction, that marital rape cannot happen, or that power held by a male employer is not a relevant part of a situation in which he may be sexually suggestive to his female employee."[14] As hooks states, "Ideologically, most of us have been raised to believe that war is necessary and inevitable. In our daily lives, individuals who have passively accepted this socialization reinforce value systems that support, encourage, and accept violence as a means of social control."[15]

Furthermore, "for political leaders and citizens alike, the military offers an appealing and rational model for society, especially when society is threatened by crime and disorder. Accordingly, the mainstream accepts the military model and metaphor in criminal justice as well as society as a whole because together they represent a sense of order, safety, and protection."[16] Perhaps this partly explains why we do not look at militarism to explain social phenomena. It is so pervasive that our awareness of its presence is dulled.

For some, however, the impact of militarism on women is all too apparent. As Enloe tells us, "Militarism depends on distorted government budgets, but it also depends on the public denial or trivialisation of wife battering, rape and pornography."[17] Virtually by default, acceptance and reward of masculine characteristics lead to rejection and scorn of feminist issues. On 17 January 1999 the CBS show "60 Minutes" aired a segment on domestic violence in the military, reporting that in the previous five years alone there were over fifty thousand cases of females being battered by male soldiers. The report went on to note the difficulty victims of soldier battering have in seeking justice. Cases reported to military authorities, according to the news program, overwhelmingly result in no official action taken against the soldier. Women who were battered reported on the difficulty their men seemed to have in leaving their war preparedness at work. What better example might we have of the connection between militarism and the harms perpetrated against women?

Any thorough study of crime incorporates an examination of social institutions, such as the family, education, politics, and economics. Clearly, the institution of militarism needs to be included in such studies. Yet militarism cannot be presented as a simple concept. While there are core features to militarism, it does have numerous forms and instances, an additional reason for examining its potential impact on criminology and criminal justice. As Cuomo expresses, war (militarism) is not just an event, it is a significant presence in society.[18] Enloe noted that militarization "usually involves confusion and mixed messages. On the one hand, it requires the participation of women as well as men. On the other hand, it is a social reconstruction that usually privileges masculinity."[19] Only by incorporating militarism into our analyses of social phenomena, with attention to its complexity, can we come to understand the impact it may have. Linking the study of militarism to feminism helps point out the myriad ways in which militarism affects people's lives.

"Many of our contemporary global crises—such as environmental pollution and the threat of nuclear holocaust—are the result of the emphasis a dominator system places on so-called masculine values of conquest and domination."[20] As Grier notes, "worldwide military priorities leave social programs in the dust."[21] In 1986 the nations of the world, on average, spent $30,000 per soldier. At the same time, in terms of education, they spent an average of $455 per child. Social programs everywhere seem to take second place to military spending. As Ruth Sivard states, "Militarization has made further inroads into a world economy already overburdened by weapons of mass destruction, poverty, and debt."[22] As Eisler and Loye put it: "In the United States almost 60 percent of every tax dollar has gone to financing foreign intervention, nuclear weapons, and other military expenditures, with only a fraction of it left (after interest payments on the national debt) for human services."[23] The effects of militarism are thus felt at diverse levels and in varied arenas. The harms generated by militarism include death, denial of resources to social programs, and the perpetuation of an ideology that supports violence and domination. The effects of militarism are not confined to the battlefield. The "collateral damage" of militarism is seen in the daily living of many people in the United States.

Therefore, militarism aids in the institutionalization of dominant ideology. This ideology is one that privileges power, domination, control, violence, superiority, hierarchy, standardization, ownership, and the maintenance of the status quo. As Felice notes, the image is that "each nation is surrounded by danger and must protect itself to survive, which gives rise to a preoccupation with power, particularly military power." From a militarized or "security" perspective, the world is a dangerous place. "There are few opportunities for cooperation."[24] "Current notions of security usually involve strength and force. As a society, we build walls, gates, and fences; lock people up, keeping them in or out; carry mace, buy guns, and stockpile weapons. These are all ways of separating people and maintaining hierarchies of haves and have-nots."[25] Furthermore, "militarism represents a structural choice that accords military priorities and arms spending a higher priority than meeting basic human needs."[26]

Some work in criminology has been geared toward an understanding of the similarity of processes that perpetuate harms, such as the similar processes and beliefs behind the behaviors of spanking (oppression in the parent-child relationship), battering (oppression in intimate relationships), and foreign policy (oppression of other countries). Militarism has been linked to violent harms, where domination, control, and hierarchical arrangements are ever present. Some criminologists have long desired a grand theory that would explain the world of crime. Perhaps such an understanding can be found in structural arrangements such as those discussed herein.

The Role of Feminism

According to Simpson, feminism is "both a world view and a social movement that encompasses assumptions and beliefs about the origins and consequences of a gendered social organization as well as strategic directions and actions for social change."[27] These two focal points—how things come to be (social organization) and how things are to be addressed and changed—are crucial to any examination of crime and criminal justice. We must try to understand why things are done in any particular way so we can decide whether to maintain current arrangements or change them. From a critical perspective, this is necessary, as there is no assumption of natural arrangements: things are as they are owing to an intricate set of social arrangements and actions. From a feminist perspective, most social arrangements were (and often still are) products of a view that casts women as inferior, that supports economic segregation, and that views people of color as less than human. Because of such belief systems, propagated through divisions of power, the modern criminal justice system has been deemed sexist, classist, racist, and ageist. Overwhelmingly, as studies have shown, sexism, classism, racism, and ageism affect theorizing and decision making. As feminist writers have informed us, to be a woman, to be lower class, and to be a person of color is to have three strikes against you, both in the society at large and in the criminal justice system in particular.

Before the pioneering work of early feminist criminologists, the exclusion of women from study was never taken into consideration. Research's focus on the behaviors of the lower class (according to official records) was not thought to be problematic. Study after study lumped people into categories of "white" or "black" with little attention to culture, ethnicity, or heritage. That the Division on Women and Crime was one of the first subsections of the American Society of Criminology tells us something about the impact of feminist approaches to the study of crime.[28] Studies on women and crime greatly expanded the scope of criminology. While the inclusion of such approaches has not been a simple task, it has proven to be fruitful. As with other nontraditional approaches, such as Marxism, peacemaking, left realism, and postmodernism, the conversation around crime and criminal justice has been enriched. As a discipline, our understanding of crime and criminal justice is informed by a greater variety of perspectives than ever before.

What are some ways in which criminology and criminal justice have benefited from the inclusion of a feminist perspective? Caulfield and Wonders identify five ways in which feminist perspectives can help guide both research and practice in criminology:

1. The focus on gender as an organizing principle for contemporary life
2. The importance of power in shaping social relations
3. Sensitivity to the way that the social context shapes human relations
4. The recognition that all social reality must be understood as a process, and the development of methods that take this into account
5. The commitment to social change as a critical part of feminist scholarship and practice[29]

Early research that focused on gender, power, context, process, and social change helped develop the belief that human beings are complex beings and that their behavior is not solely a function of any one particular feature. While some attention to gender roles had been addressed in earlier criminological theory (e.g., boys will be boys, single mothers will have difficulties), the work of feminists brought the importance of gender roles and gender socialization into sharper relief. Feminism does not, as a rule, suggest an exclusive focus on women. To the contrary, it suggests an attention to difference, such as how being female or male affects how one is perceived within criminology or is treated within criminal justice.

The interest in gender moved beyond criminological theorizing and moved into analyses of how women are treated as offenders, as victims, and even as workers within the criminal justice system. Anthologies, such as that compiled by Price and Sokoloff, highlight the various ways in which being female influences how one is treated.[30] We have learned that because of male power and male control, women are more likely to be battered by their significant other, more likely to be penalized for breaking out of prescribed gender roles, and more likely to be twice victimized in the cruelest of violent crime scenarios. The latter occurs when victims of rape, battering, or both are revictimized by a system where they are treated as seducers, as having asked for what happened to them, or as not being really harmed by the violent acts that brought them to the system in the first place.

The body of writing on feminism and criminology has addressed numerous topics, including violence against women, the role of legal process, disparities in law enforcement and sentencing, and the role of gender socialization. The topic of patriarchy has been explored and, more recently, the role of masculinity.[31] Some writers have explored linkages between patriarchy and militarism. As Feinman notes, some feminists suggest that "militarism and patriarchy are in effect and construction consanguine, and moreover, the antithesis to justice and peace."[32] The structural arrangements of power and control have been examined and often linked to gender socialization, with some attention to the possibly structural roots of such beliefs.[33]

This chapter does not resolve the question of whether patriarchy or militarism came first, but the readings do show that the two are intricately woven together. As Elster states, "All of [the] dimensions of patriarchy—its assumptions, its values, its divisions of labour—are crystallized and hardened in the military, the most patriarchal institution in an already patriarchal society."[34] hooks adds to the argument by suggesting that "imperialism, and not patriarchy, is the core foundation of militarism."[35] She goes on to note that support for imperialism cannot be found along the false duality of male versus female. Basch would likely take issue with hooks's point, as Basch addresses as glaringly apparent "the divergence between women's issues and state policies promoted by male leaders."[36]

Yet beyond notions of patriarchy or masculinity (often construed as maleness versus femaleness) is the support for social arrangements, support that is not heavily weighted toward either men or women. Instead, the support is found in prevailing ideology and the social arrangements that ensue. An examination of these arrangements is greatly informed by an examination of feminist utopian fiction, with attention paid to the concept of basic human needs.[37] In feminist utopian cultures, people do not think dualistically. There is "no theory of the essential opposition of good and evil."[38]

Such a belief is a beginning point in breaking down one of the inherent problems of a militaristic approach to the world, the idea that the world is essentially us versus them. In contrast to social arrangements of power, domination, control, violence, superiority, hierarchy, standardization, ownership, and the maintenance of the status quo, feminist utopian societies promote cooperation, egalitarianism, diversity, sharing, compassion, trust, interdependence, sustainability, social justice, and process orientation rather than goal orientation. As Pearson elaborates, "The feminist utopian ideal is a decentralized cooperative anarchy in which everyone has power over his or her own life. . . . The basic values of these societies are the growth and autonomy of each individual; yet individuals understand that no man or woman is an island, and all personal growth occurs in the context of relationships with others."[39]

In Marge Piercy's *Woman on the Edge of Time* we see the consequences, both positive and negative, of social arrangements. Should we choose to maintain existing social arrangements, those attendant with militarism, the future is likely to exaggerate the sexist, racist, and classist aspects of the current system. This bleak future of Piercy's novel is highly technological, people are segregated based on sex and class, and everyone is owned by the multinational corporation. Yet in the future there is also Mattapoisett, Piercy's utopian community where we see the possibility of alternative arrangements. Were we to incorporate these different social arrangements, a future where basic human needs are met is possible.[40]

In "Preventing Violence in a Structurally Violent Society: Mission Impossible," David Gil discusses the relationship of inherent human needs and social structure. When societal patterns are violent, people's inherent needs are not met and their ability to develop their full potential is thus thwarted. Inherent human needs include:

- *Biological-material needs:* stable provision of biological necessities and culture-specific life-sustaining goods and services
- *Social-psychological needs:* meaningful social relations and a sense of belonging to a community, involving mutual respect, acceptance, affirmation, care, love, and opportunities for self-discovery and emergence of a positive sense of identity
- *Productive-creative needs:* exploring one's world and discovering one's potential by participating in socially valued, productive work, in a self-directed and creative manner, and in accordance with one's talents and stages of development
- *Security needs:* a sense of trust, based on experience, that one's biological-mate-

rial, social-psychological, and productive-creative needs can be met regularly, now and in the future

- *Self-actualization needs:* for becoming what one is capable of becoming
- *Spiritual needs:* finding meaning in one's existence in the face of such ultimately incomprehensible phenomena as life and death, time and space, and origins and destinations

As Gil notes, "People can fulfill their inherent needs and develop in accordance with their potential when the values and policies of their society assure them [certain] rights." The extent to which people can meet these needs "depends largely on their circumstances of living, their relative power, the quality of their social relations, and the overall quality of life in their societies." What is needed are structurally nonviolent patterns within the institutional systems. The underlying values and policies must be conducive to the spontaneous unfolding of people's potential. On the other hand, "Values underlying the policies and practices of structurally violent societies include inequality, exploitation, selfishness, competition, and disregard for community."[41] What follows, then, is a need to examine criminal justice policy and see whether it promotes militarist values (i.e., those of structurally violent societies) or feminist values (i.e., those of structurally nonviolent societies).

Implications for Criminal Justice

To fight militarism we must resist the socialization and brainwashing in our culture that teaches passive acceptance of violence in daily life, that teaches us we can eliminate violence with violence.

bell hooks, "Feminism and Militarism: A Comment"

Criminal justice engages in a war on crime. It is no accident that we engage in a war, rather than a campaign or an effort. The rhetoric of war is the language of militarism. According to Kraska and Kappeler, militarism is "a set of beliefs and values that stress the use of force and domination as appropriate means to solve problems and gain political power."[42] As noted in 1995 by Florence, Marshall, and Ogden, militarism "has slowly and consistently extended its sphere of influence to all departments of human life. The state is still constituted primarily as if for war."[43] It is not overstating the case, then, to suggest that criminal justice has become the institutionalization of militarism in U.S. culture. Where else does one see such abject uses of force and domination in the name of problem solving? "Criminals" present a problem, and criminal justice acts to solve that problem.[44] Criminal justice uses its legitimized force and domination to remove people from their homes, confiscate their property, detain them, subject them to a win/lose approach to decision making, isolate them in confinement, and, in thirty-seven states, take their life.

Here is not the place to discuss whether or not those who have been arrested for crime should be subject to such processing. That is a separate, albeit important, discussion. The distinguishing aspect here is that when the state is presented with people accused of a crime, a choice is made, and that choice has traditionally involved the use of force and domination. And as the growing incarceration rates of U.S. facilities indicate, that choice is being used more and more, and for less violent offenders.

Criminologists have explored the roles of politics and economics regarding the ways in which criminal justice operates. Some suggest it is a battle between the "haves" and the "have-nots," that what occurs in criminal justice processing is largely a function of who has economic currency and who does not.[45] Others suggest it is a largely political process, where those without political clout (who also happen to be the have-nots more times than not) are more likely to be subjected to the criminal justice system's approach. Still others suggest that the influence of patriarchy has led to a criminal justice system where women's needs are either ignored or poorly addressed. Some even suggest that the violence that befalls women is a political act owing to the state's unwillingness to act in the best interest of women, such as through the lack of appropriate laws or the lack of enforcement of existing laws.[46]

All of these claims have legitimacy. What is missing is an examination of what they hold in common. Whether for economic, political, racist, or sexist reasons, the common thread is that in each scenario, certain people are being denied fairness because of a system that dominates others so that the few may prosper.[47] Here is where an examination of militarism becomes advantageous. As Welch points out, "The military model and metaphor in criminal justice reflect the larger social forces that tend to order society. Arguably, the military model is used by the state as a template for shaping the order as well as the stratification of society, thereby reinforcing class divisions through coercive mechanisms."[48]

How, then, is an examination of feminism and militarism relevant to those who work within criminology and criminal justice? The relevance can be found at many levels, including theory building, law enforcement practices, courtroom dynamics, law creation, sentencing practices, and so on. It would be fruitful for those interested in these topics to examine them with both militarism and feminism as informing perspectives. To address the minute operations of criminal justice and the details of criminological theory is beyond the scope of this chapter. Instead, what is proffered is a broader review of two specific applications, correctional boot camps and mediation. In doing so, attention is paid to the role of beliefs, values, social arrangements, and possible consequences.

Correctional Boot Camps

According to Morash and Rucker, "boot camps have been used as an alternative to prison in order to deal with the problem of prison overcrowding and public demands for severe treatment." Citing Parent's survey of boot camp programs, Morash and Rucker list commonalities of such programs to be "strict discipline, physical training, drill and ceremony, military bearing and courtesy, physical labor, and summary punishments for minor misconduct."[49]

Boot camps are designed to be a form of shock incarceration, and to provide "an alternative to prison for young, first-time, nonviolent offenders, particularly drug offenders."[50] Yet a critical review of such programs suggests that the goals, values, and methods of such programs may in practice yield undesired consequences. Because boot camps are considered an intermediate sanction, there is an assumption that the "clients" of such programs are not in need of long-term supervision and, in fact, are in need of some form of rehabilitation. The long-term goal of such programs is to inculcate prosocial behavior into the lives of the young men who are sentenced to the boot camps.

Morash and Rucker raise an important point: "The very idea of using physically and verbally aggressive tactics in an effort to 'train' people to act in a prosocial manner is fraught with contradiction. The idea rests on the assumption that forceful control is to be valued." As noted in a story by *Life* magazine: "Here being scared is the point. You have to hit a mule between the eyes with a two-by-four to get his attention and that's exactly what we're doing with this Program." Furthermore, "the journalistic accounts of boot camps in corrections have celebrated a popular image of a relatively dehumanizing experience that is marked by hard, often meaningless, physical labor. The inmate has been portrayed as deficient, requiring something akin to be[ing] beaten over the head in order to become 'a man.' "[51] What follows is the assumption that alternative approaches to promoting prosocial behavior are not equally valued. In U.S. society, "both masculinity and power are linked with aggression/violence while femininity and powerlessness are linked with nonviolence."[52] Given that in the military, to fail at a task often leads to being labeled "woman" or "little girl," boot camps, by promoting military ideology, reject both women and what are labeled as female characteristics. This is unfortunate given what is known about how people learn and how they develop a strong sense of self-worth.

According to Morash and Rucker, research informs us that "learning happens only when a person feels valued and is valued, when he or she feels like a connected part of the human race. Feelings of self worth can only flourish in an atmosphere in which individual differences are appreciated and mistakes are tolerated; communication is direct, clear, specific, and honest; rules are flexible, human, appropriate, and subject to change; and links to society are open."[53] This is a far cry from the atmosphere of the correctional boot camp. In the long run, after being subjected to boot camps, offenders may be fearful, and they may even reduce their offending.[54] But at what cost? "Yelling at inmates, treating them with disrespect, and forcing them to undergo painful physical exercises may be counterproductive, teaching inmates that disrespect and verbal abuse are the keys to success in life. Such programs also value the most aggressive definition of masculinity."[55]

The idea that criminal justice policy can benefit from military tactics demonstrates the extent to which militarism has infiltrated the institution of social control. Boot camps are a logical extension of a war on crime, and of the concomitant problems that ensue with any war.

Mediation

According to Merryfinch, "Military values of hierarchy, discipline, obedience, and centralization of authority are deeply rooted in the social and political life of most states. A commitment to organized violence as the most effective way to resolve conflicts, a glorification of 'hard' emotions (aggression, hatred, brutality) and a strict channeling of 'soft' emotions (compassion, love, suffering) . . . are also characteristic of militarism."[56] A militaristic model relies on the use of force and domination, not only in the sense of war, or a physical sense of battle, but also in the creation of and alliance with theoretical perspectives. Feminism, especially feminist methodology, suggests a broader and more inclusive approach to how we know what we know and how we might pursue further knowledge. If we focus on problem solving within criminal justice, we find an area where the two perspectives seem most at odds with each other. In particular, one can compare an adversarial approach to problem solving and penalty assignment to a more collaborative approach that allows each party to play a relatively equal role in any decision making that is to occur. What one is contrasting is a process with preestablished roles, rules, procedures, and penalties with a process that defines little yet allows for a great deal of personal involvement and growth. The correctional boot camp model fits the former, while mediation is best aligned with the latter.

A specific type of mediation, transformative mediation, can help us examine the key distinctions of each approach. As detailed in Bush and Folger's book *The Promise of Mediation,* a transformative approach to mediation not only allows for individuals to resolve their own conflicts but also attempts to create a process where the goal is empowerment and recognition on the part of the disputants, rather than a clear solution to the conflict.[57] This probably sounds problematic to many; after all, isn't a solution to the problem the desired goal? It is because of the seemingly contradictory nature of transformative mediation that it fits so nicely with feminist theory and methodology.

Feminist approaches, by and large, do not suggest a particular way of doing things. For example, feminist methodology allows for multiple voices, multiple perspectives, and less of what is ascribed as clear, empirical outcomes.[58] Such is the nature of a transformative approach to mediation. As in other forms of mediation, the mediator is a third-party neutral with a clear role to play. However, the difference is found in the approach taken by the mediator. The mediator is trained to follow rather than lead the disputants, and to find points of recognition and empowerment, emphasize those points, and ask the disputants where they next want to go. The goal is that parties will find ways to empower themselves, especially through decision-making choices, and also recognize the perspectives of the person with whom they are in conflict. Transformative mediation is thus radically different from a community-based facilitative model of mediation (and certainly different from court-based mediation or arbitration). It also belies the assumed necessity of an adversarial model.

Criminal justice approaches to crime are predominantly based on the use of force and domination. Granted, there are exceptions, such as the courtroom work group, the use of neighborhood liaison officers, and the balancing of prisoners' needs with the needs of prison management. But the process of law itself is predicated on a rights-based model.[59] Within this model, the assumption is made that people know in advance what sanctions should be assigned to specific harms. Even with all the work that has been done in the area of victim rights, the system still pursues this prospective, rights-based model.

In contrast, as Tifft tells us, is the possibility of a retrospective, needs-based model.[60] Here we would not presume to know ahead of time how best to meet the needs of an injured person. This is perfectly in line with a transformative approach to mediation (and justice). It is also in line with feminist perspectives on harm.

Researchers in the areas of rape and battering came to learn that physical abuse is not a necessary aspect of violence. Violence against women is manifested in many ways, and we need to pay more attention to what women say about their experience, rather than rely on imposed constructs of harm.[61] What we learn from this research is that prospective, legally created, rights-based approaches to justice may be forceful, dominate the criminal justice landscape, and create clear images of who is in charge. What such approaches do not do, for many victims, is "make things right."[62]

Methods of transformative justice are clear examples of a need to move away from militaristic approaches to criminal justice. Yet it would be contradictory to the purpose of this chapter to pit feminism against militarism as a framework for criminal justice. A key feature of a nonmilitaristic stance is that one is not trying to best the other. Would use of a feminist model be beneficial to either criminology or criminal justice? In this author's mind, yes. Would feminism be a panacea for criminology or criminal justice? Certainly not. What we learn from the comparison of the two is that there are consequences to our choices.

Some scholars may wish to address the question of how militarism has influenced criminal justice historically. Others may wish to examine the degree to which militarism is embedded in criminological theory and practice. And there are those who will wonder whether the influence of militarism today is stronger or weaker than in the past. These are all interesting questions. However, for this author, what is clear is that militarism is present and its influence is growing. If we do not look at militarism and criminal justice, we will not be able to stem the tide of the growing militarization of U.S. society. If our current criminal justice system is demonstrably militarized, and if militarization can be seen to create rather than reduce harm, then it is incumbent upon criminological scholars to address militarization, its consequences, and available alternatives.

Conclusion

As I noted at the outset, I am an antimilitarist, a feminist, and a peace activist. From this viewpoint, the greatest difficulties with the current criminal justice process center on the use of violence in an attack against violence. When one goes to war against crime or violence and uses a military model to do so, what gets modeled is that violence is acceptable, so long as it is done by the "good guys." This is at the center of why people support war as a necessary and acceptable evil. While we may curse the enemy who kills our child, we simultaneously cheer our soldier who kills someone else's son.

What I believe we can learn most from looking at feminism and militarism is that militarism creates benefits for only some people. As feminist and antiwar writers have noted, the benefits of war are not accrued by the majority of the population. Instead, they may aid the oil industry (e.g., the Persian Gulf War), they may remove democratically elected governments so that U.S. interests can gain access to land and labor (e.g., the many wars against Central and South American countries), and they may be fruitless efforts in which a strong country refuses to admit weakness (e.g., the Vietnam War). Women have consistently fared less well under a military model than have men.

As we learned during the Persian Gulf War, women oppose war to a far greater extent than do men. Prior to the firing of weapons in the Persian Gulf, 72 percent of women in a Harris poll opposed a U.S. attack on Iraq, while only 48 percent of men opposed such an attack. In response to these differences of support, Harris suggests that "women have traditionally been more concerned about the human cost of war than men."[63] There is truth in this statement, to be sure. War, and the armaments of war, are the practices and monuments of men. As Enloe tells us: "there are those people, largely women, who are most hurt when social programs . . . are cut back in order to satisfy the alleged needs of the military and its industrial supplies."[64] We see a similar arrangement even when the United States is not officially at war, and we see it in relationship to the criminal justice system. While President Clinton can get legislation passed that puts 100,000 more police on the streets, and while individual states push for additional prison construction, welfare "reform" puts more women and children at risk.

Many people do not fare well in the current system. Inherent human needs are unmet for many owing to ideology, social arrangements, and a structure that privileges the needs of the haves at the expense of the have-nots. Through the use of power, violence, segregation, degradation, exploitation, and the like, institutions continue to support the status quo. By further examining the roots of such harm, antimilitarists, feminists, and activists can work to create systems of real justice.

Notes

I want to thank Pete Kraska for encouraging me to continue this conversation and for being supportive of my struggle to have it. I also want to thank my friends Dale Anderson and Larry Tifft, who have provided guidance and insight and have encouraged my pursuit of peaceful solutions.

1. Richard Quinney, "Criminology as Moral Philosophy, Criminologist as Witness," *Contemporary Justice Review* 1 (1998): 347–64.
2. David G. Gil, "Preventing Violence in a Structurally Violent Society: Mission Impossible," *American Journal of Orthopsychiatry* 66 (1996): 77–84.
3. bell hooks, "Feminism and Militarism: A Comment," *Women's Studies Quarterly* 3 and 4 (1995): 58–64.
4. Harold E. Pepinsky and Richard Quinney, *Criminology as Peacemaking* (Bloomington: Indiana University Press, 1991).
5. Patrick M. Regan, *Organizing Societies for War: The Process and Consequences of Societal Militarization* (Westport, Conn.: Praeger, 1994), 4–5.
6. Regan, *Organizing Societies for War,* 5.
7. Regan, *Organizing Societies for War,* 5.
8. Ilene R. Feinman, *Citizenship Rites: Feminist Soldiers and Feminist Antimilitarists* (New York: New York University Press, 2000), 45, 11.
9. Eric Carlton, *War and Ideology* (Savage, Md.: Barnes and Noble, 1990), 21.
10. William F. Felice, "Militarism and Human Rights," *International Affairs* 74 (1998): 25–40.
11. Lesley Merryfinch, "Militarization/Civilianization," in *Loaded Questions: Women in the Military,* ed. Wendy Chapkis (Amsterdam: Transnational Institute, 1981), 81–97.
12. Larry L. Tifft and Lynn Markham, "Battering Women and Battering Central Americans: A Peacemaking Synthesis," in Pepinsky and Quinney, *Criminology as Peacemaking,* 114–53.
13. Dorie Klein, "Violence against Women: Some Considerations Regarding Its Causes and Its Elimination," *Crime and Delinquency* 27 (1981): 64–80.
14. Hollis Wheeler, "Pornography and Rape: A Feminist Perspective," in *Rape and Sexual Assault: A Research Handbook,* ed. Ann W. Burgess (New York: Garland, 1985), 375.
15. hooks, "Feminism and Militarism," 63.
16. Michael Welch, *Punishment in America: Social Control and the Ironies of Imprisonment* (Thousand Oaks, Calif.: Sage, 1999), 122.
17. Cynthia Enloe, *Does Khaki Become You? The Militarization of Women's Lives* (Boston: South End Press, 1983), 209.
18. Chris J. Cuomo, "War Is Not Just an Event: Reflections on the Significance of Everyday Violence," *Hypatia: A Journal of Feminist Philosophy* 11 (1996): 42–54.
19. Cynthia Enloe, "Feminism, Nationalism, and Militarism: Wariness without Paralysis?," in *Feminism, Nationalism, and Militarism,* ed. Constance R. Sutton (Arlington, Va.: Association for Feminist Anthropology/American Anthropology Association, 1995), 27.

20. Riane Eisler and David Loye, *The Partnership Way: New Tools for Living and Learning, Healing Our Families, Our Communities, and Our World* (San Francisco: HarperSanFrancisco, 1990), 56.
21. Peter Grier, "Worldwide, Military Priorities Leave Social Programs in the Dust," *Christian Science Monitor,* 4 December 1986, 4.
22. As cited in Grier, "Worldwide," 4.
23. Eisler and Loye, *The Partnership Way,* 56.
24. Felice, "Militarism and Human Rights," 32.
25. Gwyn Kirk, "Women Oppose U.S. Militarism: Toward a New Definition of Security," in *Gender Camouflage: Women and the U.S. Military,* ed. Francine D'Amico and Laurie Weinstein (New York: New York University Press, 1999), 237.
26. Felice, "Militarism and Human Rights," 26.
27. Sally S. Simpson, "Feminist Theory, Crime, and Justice," *Criminology* 27 (1989): 605–31.
28. I am not suggesting that the authors of these early studies necessarily saw themselves as feminist. Although the feminist label may not be present, the work clearly advances a feminist agenda. See Susan L. Caulfield and Nancy Wonders, "Gender and Justice: Feminist Contributions to Criminal Justice," in *Varieties of Criminology: Readings from a Dynamic Discipline,* ed. Gregg Barak (Westport, Conn.: Praeger, 1994).
29. Caulfield and Wonders, "Gender and Justice," 215.
30. Barbara R. Price and Natalie J. Sokoloff, *The Criminal Justice System and Women: Offenders, Victims, and Workers* (New York: McGraw-Hill, 1995).
31. See, for example, James W. Messerschmidt, *Masculinities and Crime* (Lanham, Md.: Rowman and Littlefield, 1996).
32. Feinman, *Citizenship Rites,* 11.
33. See, for example, Tifft and Markham, "Battering Women."
34. Ellen Elster, "Patriarchy," in Chapkis, *Loaded Questions,* 15.
35. hooks, "Feminism and Militarism," 61.
36. Linda Basch, "Introduction: Rethinking Nationalism and Militarism from a Feminist Perspective," in Sutton, *Feminism, Nationalism, and Militarism,* 4.
37. The use of the word *utopian* should not be taken to mean "unattainable." Instead, some of this work is labeled *dis-utopian,* so as to emphasize the real possibility of manifesting alternative visions.
38. Carol Pearson, "Beyond Governance: Anarchist Feminism in the Utopian Novels of Dorothy Bryant, Marge Piercy, and Mary Staton," *Alternative Futures* 4 (1981): 126–35.
39. Pearson, "Beyond Governance," 126–27.
40. Marge Piercy, *Woman on the Edge of Time* (New York: Fawcett Crest, 1976).
41. Gil, "Preventing Violence," 78–79, 80.
42. Peter B. Kraska and Victor E. Kappeler, "Militarizing American Police: The Rise and Normalization of Paramilitary Units," *Social Problems* 44 (1997): 1–18.
43. Mary S. Florence, Catherine Marshall, and C. K. Ogden, *Militarism versus Feminism: Writings on Women and War* (London: Virago, 1995), 113.
44. I place the word *criminals* in quotes because my perspective is that "criminals" are socially constructed. People who are processed by the criminal justice system are not necessarily more criminal than others; what we do know is that they have, for a variety of reasons, been processed by the criminal justice system and labeled as "criminals."
45. See, for example, Jeffrey Reiman, *The Rich Get Richer and the Poor Get Prison* (New York: Wiley, 1984).
46. See, for example, Susan L. Caulfield and Nancy A. Wonders, "Personal AND Political: Violence against Women and the Role of the State," in *Political Crime in Contemporary America: A Critical Approach,* ed. Kenneth D. Tunnell (New York: Garland, 1993).
47. Anarchism raises similar issues about how a system dominates others. We can learn a lot from anarchist perspectives on the long history of existing practices and the need to make radical changes in both structure and belief if we are to truly live as humans. See, for example, Larry L. Tifft and Dennis Sullivan, *The Struggle to Be Human: Crime, Criminology, and Anarchism* (Orkney, U.K.: Cienfuegos, 1980). Whereas anarchist perspectives are typically cast as anti-American and decidedly communistic, militarism has no such

artificially created ideological boundaries and therefore may be more acceptable to those who could participate in this conversation.

48. Welch, *Punishment in America,* 122.
49. Merry Morash and Lila Rucker, "A Critical Look at the Idea of Boot Camp as a Correctional Reform," *Crime and Delinquency* 36 (1990): 205.
50. Joel Samaha, *Criminal Justice* (Belmont, Calif.: Wadsworth/Thompson Learning, 2000), 382.
51. Morash and Rucker, "A Critical Look," 214, 206.
52. James W. Messerschmidt, *Capitalism, Patriarchy, and Crime: Toward a Socialist Feminist Criminology* (Totowa, N.J.: Rowman and Littlefield, 1986), 59.
53. Morash and Rucker, "A Critical Look," 213.
54. Actually, research suggests that boot camps are no more effective than other sanctions. In fact, in some locations, boot camp graduates had worse recidivism rates than those who were sentenced to regular parole or prison. See, for example, Samuel Walker, *Sense and Nonsense about Crime and Drugs: A Policy Guide* (Belmont, Calif.: West/Wadsworth, 1998).
55. Walker, *Sense and Nonsense,* 219.
56. Merryfinch, "Militarization," 9.
57. Robert A. Baruch Bush and Joseph P. Folger, *The Promise of Mediation: Responding to Conflict through Empowerment and Recognition* (San Francisco: Jossey-Bass, 1994).
58. See, for example, Liz Stanley and Sue Wise, *Breaking Out: Feminist Consciousness and Feminist Research* (London: Routledge and Kegan Paul, 1983), and Mary F. Belenky, Blythe M. Clinchy, Nancy R. Goldberger, and Jill M. Tarule, *Women's Ways of Knowing: The Development of Self, Voice, and Mind* (New York: Basic, 1986).
59. See, for example, Larry L. Tifft, "The Coming Redefinition of Crime: An Anarchist Perspective," *Social Problems* 26 (1979): 392–401.
60. Tifft, "The Coming Redefinition of Crime."
61. See, for example, Neil M. Malamuth, "The Mass Media and Aggression toward Women: Research Findings and Prevention," in Burgess, *Rape and Sexual Assault*; Klein, "Violence against Women"; and Stanley and Wise, *Breaking Out.*
62. See Daniel Van Ness and Karen Heetderks Strong, *Restoring Justice* (Cincinnati: Anderson, 1997), and Howard Zehr, *Changing Lenses: A New Focus for Crime and Justice* (Scottsdale, Pa.: Herald, 1990).
63. Louis Harris, "The Gender Gulf," *New York Times,* 12 December 1990, A19.
64. Enloe, *Does Khaki Become You?,* 207.

9

Playing War

Masculinity, Militarism, and Their Real-World Consequences

Peter B. Kraska

Most of us have seen those archived films of Adolf Hitler in front of thousands of soldiers and tanks ranting about the virtues of military might and superiority. It is easy to conclude that German culture during the Nazi era was imbued with militarism. Unfortunately, lofty-sounding concepts such as "militarism" run the risk of seeming too far removed from today's American society. Demonstrating that militarism remains a potent contemporary cultural force requires a little more work.

One of the best avenues for showing its relevance is to examine popular culture. A graduate student recently exposed me to a fascinating slice of militarized popular culture in one genre of rap music. She found lyrics from rap musicians such as "Mystical f" and "Master P" that were steeped in militarism—referencing correctional boot camps, tanks in the ghetto, gang members as soldiers, police as an occupying army, and police-gang conflict as war.[1] This language, combined with the visual imagery on their web pages, struck a familiar chord. In working on the Oklahoma City bombing case (*Timothy McVeigh v. U.S. Government*), I was introduced to a similar militarized subculture among right-wing militia groups. This militarism also permeated the police operations of the initial and final raids of the Branch

Davidian residence in Waco, Texas—the same governmental operation Mc-Veigh was attempting to avenge.

These real-world examples show us that studying and exposing militarism as popular culture is best done hands-on. This chapter presents a description and analysis of my firsthand experiences with militarized culture during a two-year ethnography of rural police officers and military soldiers working in collaboration to form multijurisdictional Special Weapons and Tactics (SWAT) teams, referred to from now on as "police paramilitary units" or "PPUs." The objectives of this chapter are to demonstrate: (1) the direct relevance of militarized culture to the study of criminal justice; (2) the seductiveness and embeddedness of militarism in modern American society; (3) how traditional themes of masculinity are an integral part of militarized culture; and (4) the links between the micro (personal experience and identity) and the macro (macropolitical and social implications).

As the reader will discover, my struggle in conducting this ground-level research had little to do with any inability to develop an understanding of the subjects; the disturbing aspect was the ease with which I succeeded. The macropolitical and social implications of this research event should alarm most readers. On a personal level, what disturbed me most was how I, a person who had so thoroughly thought out militarism, could have so easily enjoyed experiencing it. This study illustrates the expansive and seductive powers, even in these "postmodern" times of sanitizing and condemning all that is "violent," of a deeply embedded ideology of violence and its accomplice, hypermasculinity.

Playing Warrior

I was invited to observe an ad hoc "training session" of police officers and military soldiers. This was an "ask no further questions" invitation; my attempt to gain more information resulted only in vague references to "tactical operations training." Despite my discomfort, I knew this was a good opportunity to meet police officers who were also military soldiers in the National Guard or military reserves. As part of my research into the emerging relationship between police and military forces in the post–Cold War era, I welcomed the chance to witness the overlap firsthand.

I knew two of the participants well (I refer to them here as "Mike" and "Steve"). Over the course of a year we had developed a casual relationship that included numerous in-depth conversations and approximately sixty hours of fieldwork. With this groundwork laid, the scenario described here was my first experience with Mike and Steve that included their police and soldier acquaintances. Mike and Steve were excellent informants because of their amiable personalities and their awareness of the broader implications of their activities. They also filtered the world through a peculiar set of presuppositions. Both of these highly trained soldiers completely lacked respect for the military bureaucracy, disdained the government as an institution (although, as the bumper sticker says, they "loved their country"), and had an attitude of irreverence toward authority and mainstream society that would make any good leftist smile. At the same time, they were highly respected and trusted within the military, and they revered military weaponry and tactics. Both were serving in the military reserves.

I arranged to meet my informants at a supermarket parking lot. They motioned me excitedly to the trunk of their car, removed several black canvas attaché cases, assured me that all of this was legal, and showed me several semiautomatic and fully automatic military weapons. Most of the weapons were actually owned by the military and had been lent to these soldiers over the weekend for "training." The men were eager to get to the "training site" and insisted, despite my protests, that I ride with them.

On the ride to the site, I asked Mike and Steve about their connection to training police officers. They explained that they worked regularly with several different departments interested in tactical operations. These officers either served currently on a tactical operations team (commonly referred to as SWAT) or were attempting to create such a team. The group we were meeting, they continued, included two ex-military soldiers who were also in the reserves. They had just begun to organize an "emergency response unit" (a police paramilitary unit) that would include selected officers from several small police departments. These officers strongly believed that small municipalities and county police were being left behind by not having special tactics teams, even if only for contingencies. According to Mike, "This shit [creation of PPUs] is going on all over. Why serve an arrest warrant to some crack dealer with a .38? With full armor, the right shit [pointing to a small case that contained a nine-millimeter Glock], and training, you can kick ass and have fun." True to their irreverent nature, Steve added: "Most of these guys just like to play war; they get a rush out of search-and-destroy missions instead of the bullshit they do normally."

The training site was an unregulated piece of land containing a vertical, eroded hillside, which made an ideal backdrop for stopping bullets. Debris from previous shooting sessions was scattered everywhere—glass, water jugs, paper targets, shell cases, and household appliances. I knew this sort of setting well. As a youth, having lived all over the country, it seemed to me that every community had somewhere an abandoned piece of land where the noise and destructiveness of guns were tolerated, although I suspect such sites have become less available over the last twenty years.

I followed my companions to a half circle of trucks and cars, where seven police officers were laughing and talking. Our arrival silenced their conversation, and they met my escorts with smiles and outstretched hands. Mike introduced me as a professor of policing who believed in the Second Amendment. I could tell instinctively from their looks that I needed to take the lead in defining myself to them. Although these processes were not conscious at the time, I remember that a tall, lean officer used profanity when I walked up; almost instantaneously, the "f-word" casually came out of my mouth. When they inquired into my past, I managed to mention my roots in Alaska and the fact that I had been a fishing guide in the Alaskan bush. These attempts at what Goffman calls "impression management" were only the beginning of a long performance that solidified my position in the group as "fitting in" with their normative system (conservative, adventurous, hyper-masculine, militaristic), a convincing performance that still disturbs me.[2] A quick semiotic analysis of each of these friendly men's clothes told volumes about their culture: several had lightweight retractable combat knives strapped to their belts; three wore authentic army fatigue pants with T-shirts; one wore a T-shirt that carried a picture of a burning city with gunship helicopters flying overhead and the caption "Operation Ghetto Storm"; another wore a tight, black T-shirt with the initials "NTOA" (for National Tactical Officers Association). A few of the younger officers wore Oakey wraparound sunglasses on heads that sported either flattops or military-style crew cuts.

As part of their full tactical uniforms, these officers sometimes wear Oakley brand goggles designed to fit inside their Kevlar helmets or over their "Ninja"-style hoods. During previous fieldwork, I have observed the popularity of this style of wraparound sunglasses among the younger and more paramilitary-minded officers. Their image is part of a futuristic style that emphasizes a full covering of the body, hands, and face with black or urban camouflage clothes and paraphernalia. Along with very short haircuts, these police strive for a cold, fearless, mechanistic look. The Oakley goggles, along with balaclavas, helmets, or both, as well as an array of sensory-enhancing devices for improving their hearing and eyesight, are critical to this techno-warrior image. One company labels its tactical armor as the "Cyborg 21st" line.

Steve suggested that they should line up their vehicles with tailgates or trunks facing the hillside. Once in position, each of the men laid out on mats or gun cases the various weapons and ammunition he had brought. I was awestruck, ceased to be a reflective observer, and entered the moment with fascination and alarm. Each weapon was unsheathed with care; some of the officers wiped down their already spotless weapons with silicone-impregnated rags. There were at least fifty firearms, including fully automatic urban warfare guns (Heckler and Koch MP5, MP5/40), modified tactical semiautomatic shotguns, and numerous Glock- and Barretta-brand pistols. There was also a battery of firearm paraphernalia, including noise suppressors, special-use shotgun shells, laser sights, clip-on flashlights, and, Mike and Steve's pride, a newly issued night-vision scope. I became anxious and looked around nervously, especially at the highway in our view, as if we were doing something illegal. Then I recalled a calming bit of folklore from an old Western: "Who would complain? And so what if they did? Hell, they were the law." Without reflecting on the broader implications, I felt at ease in the moment.

The men held a short discussion as to how they would go about their "training." By now I knew that the term "training" was likely the "front-stage talk" used to legitimate and professionalize this group's activities. One of the men (I'll call him "Mel") didn't participate in this discussion or in the presenting of the arms ritual. He was aloof and dispassionate; initially, I misinterpreted this behavior as apathy. Finally, once the group had reached consensus about how to proceed with the "training," Mel coolly unsheathed a Weatherby bolt-action rifle with a 3 × 9 power scope, walked diagonally another 150 yards from the vehicles, and set his weapon on a six-foot-long mat with a small bipod. I realized then that Mel, who had quite a bit of experience in "tactical operations" in the military and police, was the sniper.

I didn't recognize the high status of the sniper position until I later began to read about elite special forces units within the military. Police paramilitary units are to policing what the Navy Seals or Army Rangers are to the military. These small cadres of warriors delineate each member by some special skill or expertise. Many police paramilitary units now have, for example, one member who is an expert in the sort of explosives that allow quick entry into a "fortified" residence. The military and police special operations subculture holds the sniper in especially high reverence. The subculture glorifies the skill, discipline, endurance, and mind-set necessary to execute people from long distances in a variety of situations. Some of the most popular items available to the police in numerous police catalogs are the videos and manuals on "sniping," usually authored by ex-military special operations snipers.

The group decided to begin by shooting pistols. For the next twenty to thirty minutes they shot at silhouettes of "bad guys," employing an array of maneuvers and tactics that required speed and skill to perform. The group was particularly impressed with Steve: he was able to draw his ten-millimeter Lock 20 handgun and rapidly fire four rounds each into three "bad guys" spaced about twenty-five feet apart. All twelve shots were deemed "kill shots"; the group found it remarkable that he managed, despite the speed with which he fired, to save his last three shots for the unseen "bad guy." Later I discovered that Steve had special status among his paramilitary policing peers, aside from his superior weapons skills, because he had served in combat in Operation Desert Storm.[3]

Next came the Heckler and Koch (H&K) MP5. My first exposure to the MPS line of weapons, of which the MP5 is part, came from an H&K advertisement in a policing magazine. The advertisement exploited the hierarchy of status in militaristic thinking with regard to "elite" military special forces units. The message was:

> This weaponry will distinguish you, just like the revered Navy Seals, as an elite soldier in the war on drugs. . . . *From the Gulf War to the Drug War.* . . . Winning the war against drugs requires some very special weapons. Weapons that law enforcement professionals can stake their lives on. The MPS Navy model submachine gun was developed especially for one of America's elite special operations units. Battle proven in the Gulf War, this model is now available for sale to the police at a special low price.

The MPS series is the pride and the staple of police tactical operations units and holds a central place in the paramilitary police subculture. Its imposing, futuristic style overshadows its utility as a superior "urban warfare" weapon. Numerous pencil drawings, paintings, sculptures, and jewelry available for sale to paramilitary police officers depict the ultimate "tactical operations" officer; the weapon of choice is almost always some version of the MP5. The popularity of these weapons is enhanced by a multitude of accessories, including laser aimers, sound suppressors ("silencers"), and training programs sponsored by H&K.

The training of police paramilitary officers by for-profit corporations appears to be a lucrative and growing industry. Paramilitary policing magazines contain advertisements from numerous training organizations. Some are restricted to police and military personnel; others admit anyone willing to pay the tuition fee of five hundred to three thousand dollars. One paramilitary training facility operated under the auspices of Eastern Michigan University. The Heckler and Koch "training division" not only trains the police in the use of their high-tech weaponry and tactics but also actively promotes the paramilitary subculture. This company commissioned an artist who specializes in drawing military special operations teams and now offers for sale twelve prints of highly detailed pencil drawings of police paramilitary forces in action. I have seen these drawings used as wall art in police departments, on police officers' business cards, and in public relations brochures.

The MP5s clearly altered the tone of this "training session." The controlled, methodical approach to firing the pistols vanished, and I realized that the pistol practice was only a prelude (or, for those who prefer a psychosexual link, the foreplay) to a less restrained form of "play." Targets filled with water and sand were placed in front of us, and for the next thirty minutes the officers fired almost nonstop except for the brief moments needed to reset targets and to imagine new ways to prove their destructiveness. I could not help noticing how "playful" and unrestrained these men were while shooting these deadly projectiles. Sharing this activity, at least within the moment, also softened the barriers between them and fostered group solidarity. They even felt compelled to bring me into their experience.

A young, small-town police officer ("Mitch"), who also served in the Army Reserves, walked over to where I was watching, presented his MP5 with outstretched arms, and said in a subtly challenging manner, "Give it a try." I tried to avoid his provocation, but both Mike and Steve gave me covert sideways jerks of their heads, urging me to go along. Once in position, Mitch insisted that I fire it on the fully automatic setting, stressing that I was a "big boy" and "should be able to handle it." I fired at a body-sized target, and, just as this officer surely anticipated, I made all the mistakes of someone who had never fired an automatic before. I held the trigger too long, and the muzzle rose after several rounds, causing me to shoot completely over the target. I emptied an entire thirty-clip magazine in a virtual flash. Everyone enjoyed this process of affirming their own proficiency in weapons by setting up the academic "egghead" for failure.

My unreflective reaction came right out of a paramilitary movie script:

"I've never shot this high-tech crap before. I prefer a good 'side-by-side' [a shotgun]." I explained that I had spent a significant part of my youth shooting and hunting with shotguns. Because Mitch had instigated this masculine game of one-upmanship, he tested my assertion by loading and handing me a Remington 1187 tactical-unit shotgun. I gave a personally satisfying demonstration of my shotgun skills, which more than proved my worth to these aspiring warriors. Tactically, as a researcher, participating in this status-legitimating contest furthered my research objectives. At the same time, however, the incident raised some troubling questions about the authenticity of my intellectual convictions and the powerful interplay between paramilitary culture and masculine ideology.

Next the group armed itself with shotguns and several boxes of odd-looking shotgun ammunition. One of the officers fired a round into a junked clothes dryer. The explosion was unbelievably loud, despite ear protection; simultaneously, a large flash was visible in the dwindling daylight. The men also experimented with other "special event" shells, including a "shredder round," which cuts the locking mechanism out of doors. After witnessing its effect on a metal file cabinet, a younger officer said jokingly that he might load up with these shells on his next crack raid.

The high-tech shotgun ammunition entertained these military and police personnel for almost an hour. During this pyrotechnics frenzy, even I ceased to connect the technology with its use on real people and their residences. The loud, bright explosions, the destructiveness, and the laughter took me back to a youth filled with bottle-rocket wars, imaginative uses of fireworks, and a tacit belief that the bigger and more destructive the explosion, the better. As with these police and military personnel, however, this fun-filled activity often was not benign. Frequently my objectives as a youth were to destroy other people's property and to terrorize despised neighbors and school officials.

I later mentioned to the group that I did not understand the utility of the high-tech weaponry aside from its recreational value. Several of the men explained that these new technologies, and tactical units in general, were mostly the result of the "out-of-control drug and crack problem." Serving arrest and search warrants and conducting drug raids in crack-infested neighborhoods, they explained, required a well-trained, well-equipped tactical operations unit. (Until quite recently, police paramilitary units have been limited to hostage or barricaded-suspect situations.) They also pointed out that these neighborhoods were "powder kegs" ready to explode. For them, tactical operations personnel were the front-line defense for the inevitable emergence of civil disturbances.

Mel concluded the "training" with an exhibition of his sniping skills. The group was awed and mentioned instances of Mel's uncanny ability to remain calm and disciplined under pressure. I never asked whether Mel had actually killed anyone as a sniper; the group's admiration of his ability and apparent willingness to kill was unsettling enough.

Debriefing after the Experience

Mel the sniper and his accompanying status coincide with long-running scripts rooted in militaristic thinking. His demeanor and training, calmly shooting "head-size" jugs of water behind plates of glass, were poignant reminders of the potential danger represented, both symbolically and physically, by these civilian police acting as military soldiers. Thus, my ethnographic experience evoked a paradox of sensations. I found myself drifting back and forth between enjoyment and alarm. I felt enjoyment when I forgot myself and became fully immersed in the intensity of the moment, unintentionally bracketing my ideological filters. Schutz believed "that in the realm of the experienced moment, meaning lies suspended for subsequent application."[4] Discomfort and sometimes alarm came at those times of broader consciousness where even split-second moments of reflection allowed for impositions of meaning. These tensions, between the moment and conscious reflection, between enjoyment and aversion, may be instructive as to the role of cultural and ideological influences in constructing our personal ideological frameworks (even our identities), and in clarifying possibilities of reconstruction.

Several aspects of the research experience, then, were pleasurable or satisfying. The most difficult confession, in view of my profeminist orientation, is that I enjoyed gaining the acceptance of a group of male police/soldiers by using hypermasculine signifiers ("Alaskan," "bush guide," "shotgun warrior," "one-upmanship"). Many of these men's worldviews were unsettling, but (outside my research objectives) I still enjoyed their approval as filtered through their hypermasculine standards and thus was left with questioning my own perceived identity.

I also enjoyed observing and using the weaponry, explosives, and associated technology. In my youth, two older brothers and I searched continually for more efficient ways to launch projectiles to destroy, vandalize, or inflict pain on someone or something. This quest ranged from hurling dirt clods, spears, and inner tubes, to shooting "wrist rockets" (slingshots), blowguns, BB guns, pellet guns, bows and arrows, and, when available, fireworks. We attempted to approximate the "war experience" by engaging in painful and often terrifying BB gun and pellet gun wars, complete with casualties. This quest for more powerful weapons peaked when we smuggled a .22 rifle out of the house and shot it in our suburban backyard with a homemade silencer. I found myself, twenty-five years later, holding the ultimate projectile-hurling technology, fitted with a "sound suppressor" that actually worked. The quest was complete.

Power played a role as another enjoyable aspect of this experience. I had an intense sense of operating on the boundary of legitimate and illegitimate behavior. Clearly much of the activity itself was illegal, although reporting it would never have resulted in its being defined as "criminal." As mentioned earlier, I felt at ease and in some ways defiant. I've had this experience in the past when field-researching police officers, and I realize that in a sense I am basking in the security of my temporary status as a beneficiary of state-sanctioned use of force. This is likely the same intoxicating feeling of autonomy from the law that is experienced by an abusive police officer, corrupt judge, or politically wired corporate executive.

Other aspects of this research experience were less disturbing. In a society that lures us into depthless lifestyles and in which a complex web of implicit regulations increasingly predetermines our choices, stepping out of the safe halls of academe into unregulated, original experience was exhilarating.[5] It was also instructive: I discovered, in unmasked form, the link between the police and military, the state's two primary use-of-force entities. Mainstream police academics routinely reassure themselves about the recent turn toward community service, accountability, and responsiveness. This research constituted a first step in realizing that the coercive dimension of policing is probably expanding alongside community policing rhetoric and imagery.

Linking Firsthand Experience with Macro Implications

At this point I contextualize my experience within its social, cultural, and macropolitical implications. Thomas notes that good ethnography "takes seemingly mundane events, even repulsive ones, and reproduces them in a way that exposes broader social processes of control, taming, [and] power imbalance."[6] With proper substantiation, then, this ethnographic study can be used as a window from which to view larger societal trends, ideological influences, and the nature of the state's construction and maintenance of power.

Police in Battle-Dress Uniforms (BDUs)

With little effort, this ethnography uncovered six police departments in a small geographical area that had established within the previous four years autonomous, fully staffed police paramilitary units (PPUs). Mike and Steve knew of five additional units in the process of forming. Fortunately, as opposed to merely hoping that the reader will consider my local experience as indicative of national trends, I followed up this ethnography with two national-level surveys of police departments serving communities of twenty-five thousand people or more. The data from these surveys demonstrate conclusively that the small-scale observations made in this ethnography mirror trends in the rest of the United States. The most immediate trend, which has gone largely unnoticed, is the growth and change in the nature of U.S. police paramilitary units since the mid-1980s.[7]

The drug war fury of the 1980s and 1990s spawned an enormous growth in the number of PPUs (see chapters 1 and 10). More important than the increase in units, however, is the almost complete reversal of their function. My ethnographic discovery—that these small-town PPUs were far more involved in conducting proactive drug raids than in the traditional "reactionary" role of SWAT teams in the 1970s (barricaded suspects, hostage and terrorist situations)—held true at the national level as well. Today about 70–90 percent of PPU activities, whether in small, medium, or large police departments, involve either no-knock drug raids on private residences or proactive patrol work in "high crime" areas. In fact, the number of drug raids conducted by PPUs has gone from about three thousand a year in the early 1980s to about thirty thousand a year by the late 1990s. Almost 18 percent of all departments serving communities of twenty-five thousand or more routinely deploy their units as a proactive patrol force.[8] Clearly, this form of militarized policing has moved from the outskirts of police operations to a normalized presence.

The Fresno, California, police are a good example. In a popular police magazine, Fresno police claim that the streets have become a "war zone"; they have responded by deploying their SWAT team, equipped with military fatigues and weaponry, as a full-time patrol unit to "suppress" the crime

and drug problem. The department has deemed the experiment an unquali-
fied success, has deployed a permanent unit, and now is encouraging other
police agencies to follow suit. "The general consensus has been that SWAT
teams working in a pro-active patrol-type setting does work. Police officers
working in patrol vehicles, dressed in urban tactical gear and armed with
automatic weapons are here—and they're here to stay."[9]

Just as the officers in this ethnography claimed, the "epidemics" of crack
and inner-city gangs are seen to justify a militarization of police operations.
Even by mainstream standards, establishing "civilian" police and clearly
delineating police and military activities and personnel have been unquestioned hallmarks of democratic governance. A central characteristic of the
participants in this research was the lack of delineation between the police
and military not only culturally but also in terms of material hardware,
technology, training, operations, and especially personnel. A clear feature
of the post–Cold War era is the increasing overlap between the military and
police (internal and external security functions) and, even more broadly,
between the military-industrial complex and the rapidly expanding "criminal justice–industrial complex."

The Military's Direct Influence

This examination of police paramilitary units is an appendage of earlier
research that examined the "police-ization" of the military rather than the
militarization of the police.[10] The military, with strong urging from the U.S.
Congress and the executive branch, has been attempting since about
1988–90 to become more "socially useful." This usefulness includes international and domestic policing activities. The social and health problem of
substance abuse, for example, was declared by presidential directive to be a
"threat to national security." All branches of the military, including National Guard units, have engaged in a full range of policing activities both
domestically and abroad.

Just as "Mike" and "Steve" train civilian police and hope to become police officers themselves, and just as the other tactical officers in their group
work for the state as both military soldiers and police, recent events in national politics illustrate the overlapping connections between the military-
industrial complex and the criminal justice–industrial complex. Attorney
General Janet Reno, for example, while speaking to a mixed crowd of military, law enforcement, intelligence, and defense industry officials, compared
the monumental effort and will demonstrated during the Cold War to the

war on crime as follows: "So let me welcome you to the kind of war our police fight every day. And let me challenge you to turn your skills that served us so well in the Cold War to helping us with the war we're now fighting daily in the streets of our towns and cities."[11]

Shortly after Reno issued this challenge, the Department of Justice and the Department of Defense agreed upon a five-year partnership to share intelligence gathering and "use of force" technology. In addition to weaponry and technology, the military and police are also being encouraged to share personnel. Just as Law Enforcement Assistance Administration money was pumped into the criminal justice system at the end of the Vietnam War, military downsizing of personnel in the post–Cold War era has brought calls for hiring more police officers. As part of the pledge to hire 100,000 new police officers, the Clinton administration passed legislation termed "Troops to Cops." Under a grant from both the Department of Defense and the Department of Justice, police agencies are encouraged to hire ex-military soldiers by providing them with five thousand dollars per "troop" turned "cop."

Warrior Culture

As illustrated by the "Operation Ghetto Storm" T-shirt worn by one of the officers in this research, the militaristic nature of the discourse on crime and drug control constitutes more than ineffectual media and political rhetoric. Filtering solutions to such complex social problems through the "war" metaphor helps to structure our values-in-use, our theories, and most important, our actions.[12] Consider how the metaphor and associated discourse of war have materialized in urban and small-town police departments deploying paramilitary police groups to patrol U.S. neighborhoods and conduct no-knock drug raids.

As noted above, the value and belief system that underpins these phenomena is militarism. Ironically, criminology as a whole has not employed this concept to any appreciable extent, despite the obvious militaristic presuppositions underlying the operations of the criminal justice system.[13] Militarism is defined as an ideology that stresses aggressiveness, the use of force, and the glorification of military power, weaponry, and technology as the means to solve problems. It underlies the tendency of states throughout history, even those preceding industrialization and capitalism, to approach perceived problems, either external or internal, with military violence or the threat thereof.

As illustrated by my ethnographic experience, militarism does not remain encapsulated within militaries; militarization requires militarism to be an integral, everyday part of society's value and belief systems in order to provide moral support, young people as warriors, and financial support for the massive expenditures that fund the U.S. military. This militaristic dimension to culture is particularly acute in those societies that place strong emphasis on military superiority, such as the United States.

Gibson develops an instructive thesis on the consequences of a pervasive and addictive militarism in recent U.S. popular culture. In referring to what he terms the "New War Culture," Gibson explains the resurrection of martial culture during the 1980s and 1990s as a reaction to losing the Vietnam War: "It is hardly surprising, then, that American men—lacking the confidence in government and the economy, troubled by the changing relations between the sexes, uncertain of their identity or their future—began to *dream,* to fantasize about the powers and features of another kind of man who could retake and reorder the world. And the hero of all these dreams was the paramilitary warrior."[14] Through film, politics, media, and field research Gibson documents how the new culture of paramilitarism, which emphasizes the lone warrior or small, elite groups of fellow warriors, pervaded young males' minds during the 1980s.

This pervasive ideology of paramilitarism certainly helps make sense of my ethnographic experiences by providing the larger cultural context from which to situate Mike's, Steve's, and the rest of the group's paramilitary praxis. It also explains the contemporaneous rise in police paramilitary units within federal and local law enforcement agencies, and the strong streak of paramilitarism found in American popular culture during the 1980s and 1990s—most obviously seen in right-wing militia and hate groups, urban gangs, and a host of recreational products based on paramilitary themes (e.g., movies, computer games, and paint-ball munitions).

As shown by my reaction to the MP5 scenario, hypermasculinity is an integral element in the makeup of militarism. "In most cultures that we know about, to be manly means to be a potential warrior."[15] The interwoven scripts of militarism and masculinity provide the cultural foundation for organized forms of violence by militaries and police, and these taken-for-granted scripts furnish a more diffuse but still pervasive social network of threatened and real violence among individual men. In a sense, then, my research experience was merely a continuation of centuries of previously scripted masculine thinking and power building—a history of militarized praxis still vital today, albeit in less recognizable forms, and one in which I reemerged as a participant.

Conclusion: Playing War, Waco, and the Oklahoma City Bombing

This ethnography illustrates the powerful and enduring nature of militarism. My enjoyment of and effortless blending into these paramilitary rituals tapped into my own deeply embedded militarized scripts. As importantly, it provides a window through which to view broader processes of militarism and militarization as they relate to the criminal justice apparatus. The identities of Mike and Steve are products of a long-standing cultural environment, idealized during the Reagan-Bush era, which actively promotes the notion that a man's worth increases in proportion to his ability to be a warrior. This influential spirit of militarism is unmistakable in video and computer games, toys, television shows, and home videos marketed to boys. The appeal of these pedagogical devices derives from their recreational nature. As with my own ethnographic experience, militarism is enjoyed and embraced, as well as imposed. Through learning, enjoying, and internalizing the tenets of militarism, the personal ideological framework for many of our youth is constructed for violence and war whether with other nations, other gangs, drug law violators, or the police. Growing older, for many, only changes and amplifies the organization, the hardware, and the consequences.

Militarism has been historically and continues to be today a seductive, pleasurable, and embedded component of social life. To make matters worse, militarism and its consequences, although pervasive, are for most people taken for granted and less overt than in the past. We do have one conspicuous example available to us, however, that demonstrates the potential destructiveness of this ideology in today's society—the Oklahoma City bombing.

Although it may not be as comfortable as framing the incident as the result of a pathological individual, Mark Hamm demonstrated in his book *Apocalypse in Oklahoma: Waco and Ruby Ridge Revenged* that masculinist and militaristic themes provided the ideological fuel for Timothy McVeigh to carry out his horrific act of revenge.[16] McVeigh's T-shirt on the day of the bombing cited Thomas Jefferson: "The tree of liberty must be refreshed from time to time by the blood of tyrants and patriots." Similar cultural themes also furnished the mind-set necessary for government officials to approach the initial and final raids of the Branch Davidian residence in Waco, Texas, as a military-style operation. In fact, aside from the pervasive militaristic culture found in the BATF and FBI's elite paramilitary units, the actual U.S. Armed Forces itself were directly involved in the planning of the Waco debacle.[17]

Hamm establishes that McVeigh was filtering his actions through the masculinist and very American theme of "revenge" when carrying out his militarized response to the government's militarized actions at Waco and Ruby Ridge. This means that McVeigh's crime occurred in a cultural context not unknown to us all. Situating such a gruesome act within these central features of American culture, however, is likely a jagged pill for most of us to swallow. The point is not to minimize McVeigh's culpability but, rather, to illustrate that my experiences with Mike and Steve, the government's actions in Waco, McVeigh's actions in Oklahoma City, the wars on crime and drugs, and the unrestrained growth of the criminal justice industry are all expressions of the same long-standing cultural pattern.

Notes

This chapter is a revised version of "Enjoying Militarism: Political/Personal Dilemmas in Studying U.S. Police Paramilitary Units," *Justice Quarterly* 13, no. 3 (1996): 405–29.

1. My thanks to Amy Nance, a graduate student at Eastern Kentucky University, who completed a fascinating research project that juxtaposed urban gang militaristic culture with militarized police culture.
2. Erving Goffman, *The Presentation of Self in Everyday Life* (London: Allen Lane, 1959).
3. Steve embodied the ultimate warrior in that he had experienced war firsthand and, more important, had killed. Killing in combat is the ultimate mark of military bravado. Interestingly, Steve never discussed having killed an Iraqi soldier as far as I knew. Everyone simply assumed he had done so because of his combat role in the war and because of his silence on the matter.
4. Alfred Schutz, *The Phenomenology of the Social World* (Evanston, Ill.: Northwestern University Press, 1967).
5. With regard to "depthless lifestyles," see Chris Rolek and Brian S. Turner, *Forget Baudrillard?* (New York: Routledge, 1993). On the ascendance of the regulatory society, see Ben Aggerne, *Discourse of Domination: From the Frankfurt School to Postmodernism* (Evanston, Ill.: Northwestern University Press, 1992); Herbert Marcuse, *One-Dimensional Man* (Boston: Beacon, 1964); George Ritzer, *The McDonaldization of Society: An Investigation into the Changing Character of Contemporary Social Life* (Thousand Oaks, Calif.: Pine Forge, 1993).
6. Jim Thomas, *Doing Critical Ethnography* (Newbury Park, Calif.: Sage, 1993).
7. See Peter B. Kraska and Victor E. Kappeler, "Militarizing American Police: The Rise and Normalization of Paramilitary Units," *Social Problems* 44 (1997): 1–18; Peter B. Kraska and Louis J. Cubellis, "Militarizing Mayberry and Beyond: Making Sense of American Policing," *Justice Quarterly* 14 (1997): 607–29.
8. Kraska and Cubellis, "Militarizing Mayberry."

9. Charles D. Smith, "Taking Back the Streets," *Police* 19 (1995): 36, 82, 16. The SWAT team in Chapel Hill, North Carolina, conducted a large-scale crack raid of an entire block in a predominantly African American neighborhood. The raid, termed "Operation Redi-Rock," resulted in the detention and search of up to one hundred people, all of whom were African American. Whites were allowed to leave the area. No one was ever prosecuted for a crime. See *Barnett v. Karpinos,* 460 S.E. 2d 208 (N.C. App. 1995).

10. See Peter B. Kraska, "Militarizing the Drug War: A Sign of the Times," in *Altered States of Mind: Critical Observations of the Drug War,* ed. Peter B. Kraska (New York: Garland, 1993), 159–206; Richard Quinney, *Criminology* (Boston: Little, Brown, 1975).

11. National Institute of Justice, "Technology Transfer from Defense: Concealed Weapon Detection," *National Institute of Justice Journal* 229 (1995): 1–6.

12. See George Lakoff and Mark Johnson, *Metaphors We Live By* (Chicago: University of Chicago Press, 1980); Gareth Morgan, *Images of Organization* (Beverly Hills, Calif.: Sage, 1986).

13. The major exception is Richard Quinney, who employed the military metaphor as an ideological referent for critiquing the criminal justice system. Quinney's original connection of military with criminal justice ideology continues today in "peacemaking" criminology; see Harold E. Pepinsky and Richard Quinney, *Criminology as Peacemaking* (Bloomington: Indiana University Press, 1991). One of the more perceptive and direct discussions of militarized masculinity in a criminological context is found in Larry Tifft and Lynn Markham, "Battering Women and Battering Central Americans: A Peacemaking Synthesis," in *Criminology as Peacemaking,* ed. Harold E. Pepinsky and Richard Quinney (Bloomington: Indiana University Press, 1991), 114–53.

14. See James W. Gibson, *Warrior Dreams: Manhood in Post-Vietnam America* (New York: Hill and Wang, 1994).

15. Cynthia Enloe, *Morning After: Sexual Politics at the End of the Cold War* (Berkeley and Los Angeles: University of California Press, 1993), 52.

16. See Mark Hamm, *Apocalypse in Oklahoma: Waco and Ruby Ridge Revenged* (Boston: Northeastern University Press, 1997).

17. See R. Martz, "Marching across the Thin Blue Line," *Atlanta Journal Constitution,* 12 October 2000, B1–B3.

10

Epilogue

Lessons Learned

Peter B. Kraska

O n 15 September 2000, while completing the editing of this book, I received a phone call from Michael Mooney, a reporter from the Southern California town of Modesto. Mr. Mooney was interested in my opinion about an incident that had shocked their small community. Federal law enforcement officials were conducting a joint drug investigation with the Modesto Police Department. Federal police had requested the Modesto Police Department to deploy their SWAT team on the private residence of Moises Sepulveda to serve a federal drug warrant. During the predawn morning of 13 September, Modesto's SWAT team conducted a dynamic entry into the Sepulveda residence using a flash-bang grenade, a device that detonates with such a loud report and flash that it disorients the occupants of the house. As SWAT officers stormed through the home securing each room, eleven-year-old Alberto Sepulveda complied with the officers' screams to lie face down on the floor with arms outstretched next to his bed. Less than thirty seconds later he was struck in the back and killed by a shotgun blast from a SWAT officer who stood over him—from all indications, an unintentional discharge. After an extensive search of the residence, no guns or drugs were found; Mike Mooney told me that Mr. Sepulveda did not have an arrest record.

This series of events would not be as disturbing if it were unique. Similar tragedies have occurred in the last few years in Denver, Colorado; Dinuba, California; Albuquerque, New Mexico; Charlotte, North Carolina; and Compton, California. Granted, the number of botched raids pales in comparison to routine raids where the same event takes place with no fatalities. Police paramilitary units conduct approximately forty thousand drug raids per year across the country. Using media sources, I have collected over two hundred reported incidents of paramilitary policing gone wrong during the last five years. These are incidents where citizens or officers were injured or killed during a botched deployment. Considering the net gain for the majority of these raids—an arrest for possessing a small amount of marijuana or small-time drug dealing—it seems obvious that this extreme police tactic of home invasions by paramilitary squads poses too great a risk to citizens and the police and is not justified by the alleged crimes committed.

The *Los Angeles Times* eventually ran a story about this incident, prompting a slew of inquiries from various media outlets.[1] The Modesto Police Department also contacted me to find out what they could do in the future to avoid such tragedies. In the midst of compiling an academic book on the influence of the military and the military model on criminal justice, I once again faced the task of translating academic discourse into accessible explanations that would assist the public and criminal justice practitioners in making sense of real-world practices.

The same lesson learned from the Modesto incident is found throughout this book: numerous recent crime control debacles are real-world consequences of an increasing reliance on the culture of militarism, the military model, and in some instances the actual U.S. Armed Forces itself, for framing our nation's crime control thinking, policies, and actions. In a larger context, they are manifestations of an intensifying punitiveness and aggression found in this country's "war" on crime and drugs. Militarization and militarism are appropriate organizing concepts, therefore, for making sense of significant developments in crime control efforts in the post–Cold War era. Only an intense ideology of militarism could drive much of the police institution into believing that forced invasions of people's private residences using police units designed around the Navy Seals model for the purpose of conducting a crude investigation into minor drug law infractions are a reasonable and beneficial crime control tactic.

Certainly the officer who executed eleven-year-old Alberto Sepulveda did not intend for this to happen—and it was clear that the entire community, including the Modesto police, was devastated by this experience. Nevertheless, it was the military model that set the preconditions for this tragedy.

This war paradigm provided the mind-set and culture that perceived a pre-dawn raid on a private residence for a drug bust as a worthwhile risk. It guided an operation that included the use of flash-bang grenades, military special operations weaponry, and a search process that came directly from military protocol during a hostage situation.

Key Lessons Learned

At the outset of this book I wrote that our objective would be not only to scrutinize the military/criminal justice blur but also to strive to understand key developments in both the criminal justice system and the military. The death of Alberto Sepulveda, along with the many real-world examples found throughout this work, provides a window through which to see the consequences of this development.[2] It is fitting, therefore, to highlight a few of the more important lessons learned from each of the chapters. These include the surveillance dimension of militarization, the significance of the police/military blur, the omnipresent influence of militarism in contemporary U.S. society, and the self-serving bureaucratic growth associated with militarized crime control.

People dying during a paramilitary drug raid is an example of the coercive and violent edge to militarization; this book has also emphasized the high-tech, surveillance dimension. The chapters by Haggerty and Ericson, DeMichele and Kraska, Simon, and Dunn all accentuate the roles of high technology, science, information management, and surveillance. These forms of control, although perhaps not as eye-catching as tragedies involving overt force, are a predominant and essential feature of the militarization of crime control and the conversion of the armed forces to law enforcement. More-over, the more coercive features of militarization often work in harmony with more subtle, technology- and information-based qualities. Conse-quently, high-modern militarization, which includes domestic attempts at controlling crime, signals a level of information processing, actuarial sur-veillance, technological sophistication, and bureaucratic cooperation and integration that we have not seen before in American history.

This more subtle form of militarization is one reason that the military/criminal justice blur is not readily apparent, despite its historic significance. My hope is that these essays succeed in proving the importance of the fading distinction between police and military to the changing nature of the mod-ern democratic state. This book has established the historical and philosophical importance of maintaining a clear delineation, and demonstrated the likely consequences of what appears to be its inevitable erosion. By examining the military/criminal justice blur, we show how the mission of today's military institution is gradually "creeping" into numerous domestic functions. We also give insight into a crime control apparatus that has enlisted the services of the military and adopted a war paradigm for handling internal social problems.

This book has also illustrated the omnipresent influence of militarism in contemporary society. The war paradigm is an approach to problem solving that has an enduring appeal. The police paramilitary officers with whom I have dealt are sincere and dedicated about what they are doing, but at the same time are intoxicated by paramilitary culture and its trappings. The cultural narrative of the hard-nosed, crime-fighting warrior, donned in high-tech garb, is irresistible. As outlined in DeMichele and Kraska's essay, the main appeal of New York City's COMPSTAT model is its militaristic flavor. Simon's chapter also identifies the warrior fantasies associated with a militarized identity and effectively links it to broader trends in punishment and correctional facilities. The last two essays demonstrate the deep-rooted gender aspect of militarism by exposing its links to traditional masculinist themes. As Haggerty and Ericson point out, the military, and the cultural images associated with it, are an exemplar for the "perfect society"; one that is highly regulated, safe, rational, technologically sophisticated, and orderly. What lies at the heart of militarized crime control is the criminal justice system remaking itself in the imagined ideal of the military paradigm.

As our final lesson, the cultural appeal of the war paradigm lends itself well to runaway bureaucratic growth. This important insight is revealed throughout this work. Most people assume, and reasonably so, that the exponential growth of the crime control industry is merely a forced reaction to a worsening crime and drug problem. Consequently, few people look for alternative explanations. Various essays throughout this book demonstrate a more plausible theory: the criminal justice system is developing into an "industrial complex," similar to the military-industrial complex. As such, it seeks out and constructs new problems for its solution, actively pursues its own self-serving agenda as opposed to working toward the "public good," and works closely with an array of for-profit organizations. Put simply, growth becomes not a means to a laudable end but an end in and of itself.

Jonathan Simon, in chapter 7, contributes an important caveat regarding the nature of this growth.

One should be wary of the implication that the increasingly paramilitary features of criminal justice agencies represent a coherent and comprehensive top-down strategy. Rather, what we see happening in policing and corrections today may be a product of multiple, overlapping, and heterodox borrowings from the military of different kinds of influences by different sectors and interests within the receiving institutions. The result is more pastiche than program.

Militarized crime control is unfolding not by grand design but by bureaucratic momentum, political maneuvering, corporate interests, and individual dynasty builders. This book has had the task of weaving together the various pieces of this phenomenon—using unifying concepts, theories, and cultural themes—into what may seem to be a "grand scheme." We are able to characterize it, therefore, as a "criminal justice–military complex." It is important to realize, however, that this is only our after-the-fact attempt to develop the big picture. In the practicing world, this "complex" is developing out of a hodgepodge of highly decentralized and loosely connected processes, some of which operate at the grassroots level (e.g., the formation of small-town SWAT teams) and some of which operate at the highest levels of government (e.g., the Pentagon and the U.S. Department of Justice).

Limits to Militarizing Crime Control?

All of the lessons learned are oriented toward exposing and analyzing a trend. Of course, as academics, our focus on description, explanation, and critique is justified. Our central objective has been to illuminate important controversial developments in the criminal justice and military institutions while making sense of them using appropriate conceptual and theoretical lenses. The essays do not discuss remedies to this state of affairs or construct alternative solutions to militarized crime control.[3] The goal of our work is merely to shed light on, and help to make sense of, a significant trend in contemporary crime control. The story told in this book will not provide much hope for those seeking solutions. Perhaps our analysis will lead others to explore alternative futures.

Notes

1. R. Trounson, "Deaths Raise Questions about SWAT Teams," *Los Angeles Times,* 1 November 2000, A3.

2. We have admittedly focused mostly on negative consequences as a way to ask questions about an unexamined development. A strong argument could be made, of course, that the military model is quite beneficial for some applications. For instance, there are those rare law enforcement situations where a team of police specialists in high-risk situations (SWAT team) is needed (e.g., a terrorist or hostage situation).
3. The only exception is chapter 8, where Susan Caulfield presents a feminist alternative labeled "transformative justice."

Contributors

Susan L. Caulfield is an Associate Professor of Sociology at Western Michigan University and a community activist. Her recent publications focus on issues related to peacemaking criminology and the creation of peaceable schools. She is currently working on ways she can integrate the academic area of peacemaking criminology with community needs in the areas of violence prevention, mediation, and conflict resolution.

Matthew T. DeMichele is pursuing his doctorate in sociology from Western Michigan University. His research focuses on controversial crime control developments in late modern society. He has a forthcoming article examining the growth of police in public school systems.

Colonel Charles J. Dunlap is a Staff Judge Advocate in the United States Air Force. He holds a B.A. from St. Joseph's University and a J.D. from Villanova University School of Law. He is a Distinguished Graduate of the National War College. Colonel Dunlap has gained national recognition for his writings on the degree to which the military institution is creeping into civilian functions and the dangers associated with this trend.

Timothy Dunn completed his Ph.D. in sociology from the University of Texas at Austin. He spent four years doing field research in El Paso, Texas, studying border enforcement by the INS Border Patrol. He is currently an

Assistant Professor of Sociology at Salisbury State University, Maryland. He is the author of *The Militarization of the U.S.-Mexico Border, 1978–1992: Low-Intensity Conflict Doctrine Comes Home* (University of Texas Press).

Richard V. Ericson is Principal of Green College at the University of British Columbia. He is a member of the University of British Columbia's Faculty of Law and Department of Anthropology and Sociology. Professor Ericson has written extensively on different substantive areas of criminology, including policing, penology, and the media. He has also contributed to the theoretical analysis of risk and governance. Most recently he authored *Policing the Risk Society* with Kevin D. Haggerty. He is currently working on *Moral Risk: Insurance as Governance,* an extensive research project with Dean Barry and Aaron Doyle that examines the governmental role of the insurance industry.

Kevin D. Haggerty is an Assistant Professor of Sociology at the University of Alberta. His research interests include policing, surveillance, risk theory, crime statistics, and science and criminal justice. From 1998 to 1999 he was a postdoctoral research fellow at the Centre of Criminology at the University of Toronto, where he conducted research on the introduction of DNA testing into criminal justice. With Professor Richard V. Ericson he is coauthor of *Policing the Risk Society.* Professor Haggerty's Ph.D. dissertation was completed in 1998 at the University of British Columbia and is entitled *Making Crime Count.* It consists of an examination of the political and institutional dimensions of the production of official crime statistics and will be published by the University of Toronto Press.

Peter B. Kraska is Professor of Criminal Justice and Director of Eastern Kentucky University's Criminal Justice Program. He has published numerous articles on various aspects of militarization and militarism as they relate to criminal justice in journals such as *Social Problems, Justice Quarterly,* and *Police and Society.* Professor Kraska's research on the rise and normalization of police paramilitary units has been featured in numerous media forums including the *Washington Post, New York Times, Los Angeles Times, Economist, Atlanta Journal-Constitution,* and the "Jim Lehrer News Hour." His current research interests lie in the ascension of "no-knock contraband raids" in the war on drugs, and theorizing the growth of the crime control enterprise.

Jonathon Simon is Professor of Law at the University of Miami. He received his law degree and a doctoral degree in jurisprudence and social policy from the University of California at Berkeley. He has also taught at the University of Michigan, New York University, and Yale. Professor Simon's research deals with the transformation of regulatory and crime control strategies in advanced liberal societies.

Index

169

Index